Also by Ted Stamp

This Was Just the Way

TELL ME SOMETHING I DON'T KNOW

TED STAMP

This book is designed to provide accurate information with regard to the subject matter covered. This information is sold with the understanding that the author is not engaged in rendering legal, professional advice.

Cover design by Elena Romanchenko, Sumit Kapur, and Prita Uppal

Published in the United States of America

ISBN: 979-8366251983

For love of wondering why and how

Soli Deo Gloria

Contents

es·say (ĕs′ā′, ĕ-sā′)

tr.v. (ĕ-sā′, ĕs′ā′) **es·sayed**, **es·say·ing**, **es·says**
1. To make an attempt at; try.
2. To subject to a test.

"... the beginning of philosophy is wonder."

—Josef Pieper, *Leisure: The Basis of Culture*

What has been is what will be,
and what has been done is what will be done,
and there is nothing new under the sun.

—Ecclesiastes 1:9

The Little Things

A stranger peeking in on the scene without any context might well wonder what I'm up to—all by my lonesome smiling ecstatically into the bathroom mirror with one of those old-school, all-wire clothes hangers dangling from my throat, the curved neck of which I've just managed to loop through the pea-sized hole in the zipper of the forest-green sweatshirt with bright yellow letters that spell AUSTRALIA that my sister sent me with a box-load of candy for my forty-sixth birthday. Which took me less than ten minutes to achieve—hence, the irrepressible, self-congratulatory smile.

Potentially Interesting Fun Fact Number One: Australians call both sweaters *and* sweatshirts *jumpers*.

Potentially Interesting Fun Fact Number Two: Americans, while mostly aware that the two are technically distinguishable by appearance and definition, generally (usually unwittingly) use the terms *sweater* and *sweatshirt* interchangeably.

It's the same jumper I was wearing earlier this afternoon over my standard wintertime layer of Under Armour as I basked in the plentiful sunshine in the community room down the hall, where in typical fashion, like a turtle on a rock, I absorbed enough heat over those two hours to keep me warm the rest of the day, even until this evening—quite a bit more than comfortably warm, actually, since it's still zipped all the way up, and my apartment is always about seventy-five degrees. At any rate, it's only as I

casually pass by the full-length mirror on the back of the bathroom door and inadvertently notice the little hole in the yellow
zipper that I become aware of what I wasn't a moment before: that
the solution to my temporary discomfort very likely lies within
my power, and I happen to be just curious enough to give it a go
instead of just bearing with it for the next couple hours until my
caregiver arrives.

It's actually the kind of decision a person with limitations like
mine sometimes makes several times a day, as far as whether or
not you have the ability, patience, initiative, and determination to
try to accomplish a given task, as opposed to waiting for the next
able-bodied visitor to spare you the necessary time and energy. In
this particular case it brings to mind a concept I once learned
about on a nature show, an instinctive behavior utilized by much
of the animal kingdom, called *maximum foraging*, which operates
with a view to efficiency as to increasing the likelihood of a creature's ultimate survival. Thus, a twenty-five-foot-long shark, seeing a three-foot-long tuna twenty feet in front of it, will decide in
a moment if it's worth the energy it would take to swim that far
for such a small meal, practically a snack. Whereas if the same
tuna were just a few feet in front of it, it might decide differently.
At any rate, in my little ecosystem, where survival of the fittest
means something quite different than it does for the average
shark, I make up my mind in a moment to try to attack what might
take a lot more time and energy than I would normally care to in-
vest in such a relatively unimportant activity, despite not knowing
what the results will be even if I'm successful, since I've never
tried it.

The adventure begins when I open the front door of my apartment in order to allow myself a better angle to back my chair just
barely into the tiny entry closet adjacent to it, careful not to run
over the long plastic hose of the vacuum cleaner, intent on

reaching the aforementioned hanger—the only of its kind within my reach, mind you, and the only kind skinny enough to serve the purpose—which hangs lonely and empty and seemingly pointless just above and to the left of my view and reach, which fortunately saves me the effort of first having to remove whatever it might have been holding. Or did you assume that my possession of it was a given, something easily procured, not even worth mentioning? On the contrary, the additional clutter of broom and dustpan, space heater, a few folding chairs, and a dangling handful of jackets, scarves, and neckties add to the challenge of getting close enough. And it's a risky venture. A one-shot deal that means positioning myself at just the right angle, reaching backwards with the knuckle side of my gimpy hand to bump up against the bottom of the flimsy hanger so as to bounce it up and off the pole from which it hangs. Which isn't as easy as it might sound, given its height and the awkward angle, though the real trick, if you do manage to bounce it free, is to catch it as it suddenly, very haphazardly tumbles groundward (picture the game Plinko on *The Price Is Right*). This means quickly reacting with the same wrist and forearm to try to bobble the bare-bones triangle toward my torso, in this case fortunately causing it to land partly against my left side, partly against the armrest of my chair, at which point I reach over with my other paw to pin it against myself.

Maybe you can imagine the tempered surge of satisfaction that follows such an achievement, including a verbal exclamation that I realize should not be too exuberant. Because although this is the first necessary triumph without which I can proceed no further, I know all too well how easily the clumsy thing can fumble and flip from the apparent safety of my hands and lap to the floor, from which its retrieval will be an additional challenge I don't care to have to waste any extra time or energy dealing with.

Then I carefully drive myself into the bathroom, where the mirror is larger and the light better than in the kitchen, where, after maybe five minutes of tedious trying to thread the slender curve of the wire through the barely-larger zipper hole, I realize I'll have to angle the thing differently, flip-flopping it back and forth and upside down more than once, interlocking my forearm through the middle, even parking my chair diagonally to the mirror a couple different ways to better gauge what my major malfunction in strategy seems to be, even as I'm mindful not to gouge myself in the eye with the little hook, as my arms and hands lack the necessary coordination to handle the thing as carefully as I seem to think I can. So it is actually surprising, and then just visually funny, a few minutes later, to see the thing happen which I had only to that point visualized: the ridiculous image of the hanger dangling awkwardly and out of place just beneath my chin, where a hanger would otherwise most certainly never be seen (the oddity of which tempts me to wear it like this outside, just for the puzzled looks and comments it would surely generate). And just as before, in the closet, the bright smiling laugh of my reaction crowns the feat as I simultaneously push on the bottom two corners of my improvised isosceles lever, which glides down easily, slowing about midway, where I pause for a moment to savor the momentary gratification.

Mission accomplished.

Instant relief.

Of a sort.

What's maybe funnier about the whole project or procedure is how it hasn't even really struck me yet (that will come a little later) how completely absurd it is that it takes such protracted, concentrated effort just to unzip a sweatshirt, especially when you think back on the days when you could do the same without even really thinking about it, certainly without looking, even while driving or climbing the stairs. Another funny thing is how assured I am from the get-go that I will succeed, and, funnier still, how what began as simple curiosity, just to see if I could do it, quickly turned into an intense operation that has consumed my whole attention and focus, making me at one point resolve not even to answer the phone or door, particularly as I first attempted and repeatedly failed at the seemingly simple task, freshly determined with each new try to keep at it no matter how long it might take, no matter how irrelevant and inefficient an activity it is in relation to my ultimate fitness and survival as a creature, working the angles of the hanger with my two gimpy hands that work surprisingly skillfully for how little physical ability remains in them, basically the equivalent of a pair of oven mitts.

Potentially Interesting Fun Fact Number Three: Never underestimate how inherently competitive and dogged you are deep down when push comes to shove, even when the end toward which you have chosen to devote your time and energy means comparatively little in the grand scheme of things.

Then something else occurs to me—a cluster of somethings, actually. First, that this unorthodox experience is one that only a relative handful of souls, past or present, have ever had the need or the initiative to attempt—which makes it a kind of privilege, albeit one which most people are likely content to live without. Likewise, it is also an experience that nearly always happens behind closed doors, which means, no matter how common or profound an activity occurs, no one else will ever know about it. That is, unless the privileged one with the hanger dangling from his chest decides to cross the room to do the only thing he can to keep this strange occurrence from the fate of most of the rest of history, which is to fade into oblivion—to capture it like a photograph, to prime the pump of the relative obscurity of life with disability (though not with video, which I can't shoot myself; though if I could it might go viral), so that it might be shared beyond this room, with some who might not only find it entertaining, but possibly an unexpected source of encouragement. The kind of occasion which in almost every case gives me the chance to laugh at myself and the odd predicament I'm in, simply because I no longer have a host of abilities I once took and sometimes still take for granted.

Dare I say *fortunately* because I no longer have these abilities? Or does such a confession imperil my credibility, not to mention my sanity? Is it really possible that a person with physical limitations as extreme as mine can, and possibly should, dare to be thankful for no longer having many abilities which were once treasured, and are even sometimes, especially times like these, greatly missed? What skeptics regarding such thinking don't understand—indeed, can scarcely understand until they walk a mile, or at least a couple blocks, in "shoes" like these—is that the lessons a person learns through just such rare experiences may not be possible to learn any other way. Which is the kind of revelation that inevitably begets its share of hypothetical corollaries—for example: Should the one whose desperate prayers for needed rest be so surprised, or bellyache, if the answer happens to come through a broken bone? Epiphanies like this are not the kind of fruit that hangs so low that just any passerby can pluck at will. Rather, it's the kind that only drops in its own perfect time, which is to say not on our own timetable, or in ways we can predict, often as a result of our having passed through less than desirable experiences which we would have chosen to avoid, had it been up to us. Even several years after the infamous hour when life as I knew it changed forever in a heartbeat, the main word most people still used for what happened that rainy morning in June is tragedy. But eventually the dreary clouds of doubt, despair, and disbelief began to part, and it became plain in various ways to more and more people, including myself and those closest to me, that this initial diagnosis was clearly not true in the way that we all first thought it was.

But back to my suddenly adapted mission of speaking my unique experience into lines and paragraphs, a process clearly gathering steam more quickly than I could have guessed. Suddenly I notice how little relief the partial unzipping has allowed, though I'm determined not to worry about it until I've transferred enough from head to digital paper to capture the essence of the experience. Though in the millisecond it took to think this, a kind of primal impulse urges me that I'm now warmer than I can possibly stand for another moment, the hanger itself also nagging me with its incessant wobbling to finish the job already and let it off the hook, get it back to its lonely, virtually pointless existence in the closet (not that I don't appreciate its indispensable role in this endeavor). And so, as if to return the favor, I begin trying to zip down again, this time without the sudden rush of satisfaction as before, since oddly I'm only able to move it another inch, if that—until, being a little more careless, taking for granted that the rest of the way should and therefore must be simple, practically a given in light of my previous success, I apply just enough impatient, jerky force to enable the stiff-necked hanger to defy me and escape the little hole it took so much concentration to penetrate. And though I have clear sight of it now without the mirror and work for a few more minutes at this lower angle before getting it back through and trying to push it down again, it won't budge.

Like a sharp pain in the gut, an inconvenient truth looms large: *All that work for nothing?*

I sigh, shake my head, try again, fail, and continue writing.

Several paragraphs later, peeking down at my sorry dilemma, I remove the impromptu lever it took so much effort to procure and, with my permanently bent quad-fingers, do my best to take hold of each partly unzipped flap of sweater as though I were tear-ing it off like in some cartoon or movie, though much less dramat-ically, careful not to overstrain the zipper, which I imagine break-ing loose and costing me twenty dollars to fix. And though in the process I expend plenty of unhelpful sighing, before I know it I'm surprised to see it breaching the little seal at the bottom as the two sides come easily apart, and I smile with yet another large sigh, expecting further relief but feeling none, even after a few minutes of sitting there, pulling the sides even further apart and sort of panting with my tongue hanging out (a little over-the-top melodrama on my part, I admit).

Potentially Interesting Fun Fact Number Four: No matter how old or mature or self-sufficient you are, or think you are, never underestimate your inherent tendency to feel sorry for yourself as often as you encounter less than comfortable or con-venient circumstances, despite how insignificant your "suffering" actually is in the grand scheme of things.

And though after several more minutes I still feel almost no relief, I do feel a fair amount of satisfaction. Not just from having achieved a couple small objectives in fairly short order—not to mention having received the hopefully unforgettable insights—but from the thought that sometimes it's the little things like this that make me more acutely aware than usual of how far I've come after nearly three decades of living differently able. Or, to say it another way, it reminds me how much little things like this often used to frustrate and sometimes depress me so many years ago, which they still do now and then, though much less so.

And while it goes without saying that there will always be plenty of things that I have to wait for someone differently-able to do for me, that hasn't made me bitter, or think any less of myself, or wish things were otherwise—though I have been tempted far too often to succumb to the latter two. Not that I would refuse a complete or partial healing if one happened to come my way, whether supernaturally or through some miraculous advance in so-called modern medicine, which could obviously prove to be a wonderful help in so many ways. Or at least that's my initial thinking. But upon a little deeper reflection, you can't help but wonder how such changes, apparent no-brainers as far as your initial eagerness to welcome them, might change you as a person—your worldview, your own unique way of perceiving and pondering things, which in my case for a good while now has been shaped as much by what I can't do as by what I can, and more so for the better than for the worse. As happened, for example, unexpectedly, almost twenty years ago, when I switched from taking my sweet time pushing myself turtle-slowly in a manual wheelchair to using an electric one, which instantly, quite drastically changed how quickly I can move from one place to another, including how far I can get on my own without assistance. This change has made possible greater independence in various ways, allowing me to navigate more efficiently both indoors and out. But at the same time, gaining this ability to rush here and there more quickly has had the unforeseen side-effect of causing me to become more impatient in ways that I wasn't when getting around at a far slower pace. It's amazing, really, how such seemingly simple changes can make a drastic difference in our perspective, as anyone who has temporarily lost the ability to hear, see, feel, or move can attest.

In a similar way, if today even just my hands started working the way they once did—which is to say splendidly, miraculously—would I not almost certainly begin taking for granted many newfound abilities that I don't currently enjoy? And wouldn't that just as certainly affect how I think and go about my life, transforming my perspective and character in unexpected, even potentially unwanted ways, perhaps puffing up pride and humiliating humility? In fact, what if, in addition to those regained abilities, I happened to regain the ability to feel pain—possibly intense, chronic pain—in places where I had grown quite content with the unexpected privilege of feeling none, or next to none (that is, from the chest down)? That might well make me wish I could return to the "lesser-able" life again. Lacking comprehensive knowledge of the future, and therefore being prone to misjudge what we think is best for us, it's easy to wish our circumstances were otherwise, to think the grass would be greener if only such and such were or were not the case. Which brings to mind the time-trusted adage that never seems to lose its relevance: *Be careful what you wish for.*

If only it were more common for us to spare a few precious minutes now and then to stop and think about such things—to be thankful for the many blessings we have rather than wishing things were better yet—it might not take us so long to be pleasantly surprised by the realization that certain limitations imposed on us might actually turn out to have positive implications for our lives. However, it seems to be our default setting to think of restrictions to our present abilities and potential opportunities strictly as negatives, synonymous with inconvenience. If the choice is ever ours whether or not to allow one pesky limitation or other into our lives, will we not kick them to the curb every single time? But to what effect, on us as well as everyone with whom we interact thereafter?

There's no denying that lacking abilities you once took for granted will likely prove frustrating as you attempt to do things which were once much easier for you to do than they are now. And while such challenges are often numerous and sometimes rear their ugly heads on days when you would rather not have to deal with them, just because it may often take more time, ingenuity, patience, and perseverance than it takes most differently-able people, or than it once took you, to accomplish such things, sometimes very simple things, like overcoming a defiant zipper, you don't have to let this make you feel like less of a human being. As long as you are content with rewards in small packages, there is at the very least the satisfaction of having conquered what you set out to do, which requires more of you than it would just to leave it be and wait for the next helpful someone to save you the time and effort. Not that there's anything wrong with that. Sometimes you just don't feel like going through the struggle and frustration, while other times there's just not time. But when there is, next time you get the chance—and it really is an opportunity, if you're willing to take the bold step of thinking of it that way—do yourself the favor of putting yourself to the test and trying, even if—perhaps especially if—the challenge seems beyond your ability or likely to cost you more time and effort than you would usually care to spend on such, so long as you're not putting your safety at risk.

Speaking of which, having come this far with my now successfully opened sweatshirt/jumper, I think a moment about whether or not I should go the extra mile and try to take it off altogether, and it's not a second later that I'm tugging at one of the cuffs with my teeth, wiggling the same shoulder, the left elbow of my stronger arm, pulling again with my teeth while still wiggling, my elbow sooner than expected emerging, then my forearm, then my hand, and next it's the right side, same deal but a little more difficult since my arm is less flexible, even as I realize with an audible laugh that it's almost an hour and a half I've been at this, stubborn contra-Darwinian mule that I am, and it's perfectly possible I might get stuck like this with my arm bound up in the sleeve, unable to do anything but stare and sigh and squirm helplessly till my help comes, my pride dealt a particularly humiliating blow. But if I quit now, I tell myself, will I ever try this again? Not wanting to find out and having come too far to give up so shamefully, I cheer myself on with the thought that Miss America herself could unexpectedly barge through the door and it wouldn't distract or deter me a bit. Then I rebuke myself for such nonsense, my desperate mission apparent having temporarily short-circuited my senses. After all, who am I to reject the probably lovely, differently-able hands and fingers, more than eager to help? My goodness. What I mean to say is that this sleeve is coming off whether it likes it or not, my elbow still wiggling, sweatshirt sagging, elbow emerging, forearm, right hand, even quicker than the first—Yes! Off at last! At least mostly—still stuck behind my back and around my waist, but free from my shoulders, arms, and torso. And yet— against all odds, even after a few more minutes, I'm no cooler than before I began. But do I care? I know one thing and one thing only in this moment: I've gone head-to-head in one-on-one combat with an obstinate opponent and come out mostly on top, even while simultaneously managing to record the ordeal for posterity. What more could a guy with oven mitts for hands ask for—except maybe a friendly pop-in from Miss America?

Disillusioned

The first thing I clearly remember as we carefully navigated the congested streets of downtown Minneapolis, searching for a place to park, is the rather unsavory alley we passed through just before reaching our destination, which gave me a shudder as I contemplated someone jumping out of the shadows to rob us—a suspicion, I confess, largely due to living most of my life in a rural setting, and just as likely from having seen far too many movies and TV shows. What makes the memory so unforgettable is the unexpected sight I happened to notice beneath a loading ramp just as we neared the end of the alley: a nest of ruffled blankets that appeared to have been recently occupied. A sobering reminder of how harsh this life can sometimes be, of how much I take for granted every day, of how far from home we were, figuratively speaking. But it was a dose of reality that helped set the tone for the event my friend and I had come to see, where miracles might well take place, perhaps even for the likes of the unfortunate inhabitant of such a humble dwelling, if only he might find his way there.

Having found an indoor parking ramp shortly thereafter, which felt a little safer than parking on the street—the irony of which, in contrast to the previous image, escaped me at the time— my friend and I and an elderly friend of his embarked on the several-block trek to our destination. A brisk September evening, daylight fading fast, streams of people from all walks of life flowing both ways down the crowded sidewalk in a kind of orderly chaos. And though the three of us had discussed much of the way there what we might expect, each eager with our own unique degrees of anticipation, the atmosphere itself seemed charged, even before we got inside, perhaps partly the result of the collective energy of so many souls within close proximity, a big change from what we were used to back on the southwest prairie. It might have taken us ten or fifteen minutes to finally see the fold-up plastic sidewalk signs that said we had reached our appointed venue, the corporate name in big red letters with its familiar bull's-eye logo.

We had come to see a well-known charismatic evangelist whose unorthodox ways had repeatedly piqued the attention of my friend and me for years, as often as we happened to tune in on the only channel he ever appeared, a network known for its flamboyant, eccentric characters. It wasn't so much that we followed the man and his ministry, as that we had each been drawn like moths to a flame by the phenomenal nature of these popular gatherings and had separately reached essentially the same conclusions about him: that while to some degree he proclaimed the biblical gospel, utilizing all the expected Scriptures and terminology, the importance of that message seemed consistently secondary to the demonstration of what purported to be physical healings and deliverance ministry. Not only that, the man had a reputation for belonging to an infamous cabal of so-called "prosperity preachers" known for taking shameless, unapologetic pride in their wealthy lifestyles. And while this latter trait alone was sufficient to justify our initial reservations about him, in the interest of satisfying our ongoing curiosity as we weighed the pros and cons, we gave him more than his fair share of the benefit of the doubt.

So naturally when we heard that he was coming to Minneapolis, it seemed like too good an opportunity to pass up. Getting a closer look might be just the thing to make the difference in our discernment, we thought, and less than three hours' drive each way would be a small price to pay if it meant the chance to finally put to rest the one itching question that more or less summarized them all: Is the man a charlatan or not? Of this motive my friend's friend was unaware, which made no difference in any case. But when she learned that we were going, she wanted to come too, being herself familiar with the man, though more enthusiastically so than we, which apparently had to do with her claim to have been healed decades before by another well-known and equally infamous charismatic of similar ilk, one Oral Roberts.

After a further substantial jaunt through the large, bustling facility, the three of us found an empty spot with a decent view in the upper deck, facing almost directly across from the stage at the opposite end of the arena. Marcella, who was at least seventy-five and had been complaining almost since we left the van of her fatigue from such a long walk, was especially relieved to sit again, speaking frequently and optimistically of soon receiving her healing, especially for regular bouts of angina. Before we had time to say much else, I was surprised the next moment—though again unaware at the time of the irony—to feel on my shoulder the softly-placed hand of what turned out to be an anonymous middle-aged woman. When I turned to face her, she said something to the effect of healing and asked if I would mind if she prayed for me. Shaking my head as I bowed it, trying to focus on her words rather than the way she tenderly rubbed my shoulder as she probably quoted verses I don't now remember, asking among other things that I be raised right up out of my wheelchair that instant in Jesus' mighty name, it was hard not to imagine people staring as they passed by. Still, I believed in accord with her request, punctuating that faith with an *Amen* and a smile, though I felt nothing more than her caring sincerity as I raised my head and watched her disappear.

This didn't strike me as unusual or bother me because it's been happening ever since I've been in the chair, and the people who do it, almost invariably strangers, always mean well. In fact if I had a dollar for every time it has happened, I could treat a good friend, or maybe even that poor soul whose disheveled bed I had spotted earlier, to a nice meal. At any rate, when you're at a service of this kind you can't but expect otherwise, especially in such a metropolitan setting. At the very least this shows that, even in this late day and age so far removed from the Savior's first appearance, there are plenty of people out there who sincerely believe, as I do, that the God of the Bible is still willing and able to heal—body, soul, and spirit.

Not more than a few minutes later, a pair of strangers sitting nearby also encroached, excitedly describing how they had come the night before and one of them had been healed. She was believing for a miracle, she gestured, and a surge of power rushed through her whole body like lightning, crown to heel, which instantly restored her hearing. She hadn't been deaf, she confessed, but something wrong had been put right. This, of course, added to our anticipation as we briefly whispered about it after she floated away, though I confess the first thing that crossed my mind the moment she opened her mouth was the suspicion that she may have been planted there by the ministry in order to heighten anticipation in just such a way. And right or wrong, this suspicion was only strengthened not long after when a large cardboard bucket like you might get at the movie theater was passed in our direction, which was not full of popcorn.

After sitting for a while watching people fill the place, it wasn't long before the lights dimmed and the stage lit up—the music boomed, the audience stood and cheered with enthusiastic applause and outstretched arms, anticipation giving way to the realization that we were actually there in person rather than seeing things through the television. Back and forth the sharp-suited worship leaders paced as they led the multitude of us in song, the tempo of the first few quick and catchy, and the last few slower and more somber, meditative, the whole thing stirring your emotions accordingly, which seemed both satisfying and somewhat manipulative. Between each song, in a solemn tone spoken against the backdrop of a placid piano interlude, one of the leaders would say something about the goodness or power of God, or quote a verse or passage, or pray, and off we'd go again. And though my friend and I were primarily there on business as secret agents, testing the waters to see what passes for mainstream Christianity these days, we were still genuine followers of Jesus, eager to take the opportunity to raise our hands and voices in praise to God, and there was actually a wonderful sense of unity and fellowship among us all. This particular aspect was not entirely new to me, as I had experienced similar as part of an audience at least twice that size at a Billy Graham Crusade at the Metrodome just after I came to saving faith in Christ in the mid-nineties, and then also at a couple other Christian men's gatherings at the same locale a couple years after that, each a monumental experience you don't easily forget. But as we continued to worship, and the cardboard buckets sooner than expected made their way back to us again, the popping sound of coins thumping the bottom, the mere sight of them grieved me even more than the first time—though from the stage we were assured more than once that the Lord was moving mightily, and what a blessing it would be if we could all do our small part to help the ministry accomplish God's will in gatherings like this all over the world, India being one of the next and most prominent—tremendous crowds, meaning tremendous needs, both spiritual and material.

After maybe half an hour or more of this, the big tan kahuna with white hair and outstretched arms strode out of the shadows to center stage in his signature all-white jumpsuit and persona, even as our voices crescendoed: *Then sings my soul, my Savior God to Thee, how great Thou art! How great Thou art!* That didn't sit right either, the timing perfectly orchestrated, almost certainly not by chance. I don't remember his message, though it nearly always had some connection with the willingness and power of God to do miracles, the critical importance of faith in this regard, and the blessing attached to giving in support of such a vital ministry (the usual *plant a seed, reap a spiritual and material harvest* pitch).

Then it was time for the main attraction, the central reason we, and presumably the vast majority of those present, had come, when he invites the needy of all kinds to flood forward to receive their own personal miracle (*This Is Your Day*), and for the next ten to fifteen minutes they trickle down the aisles and spill onto the arena floor, crowding the platform on three sides. And though my friend and I had seen this phenomenon so many times before from our far-removed living rooms, it is another thing entirely to witness in person. The first time I had experienced this was at that Billy Graham Crusade, where, in response to a convicting gospel message—though one without any connection to healing except that of the sinful soul, and without any paper buckets circulating—the stream of souls poured down every aisle of every deck to the stage below, which was moving to witness and brought tears to your eyes. In fact, if on that occasion I had not already committed my life to Christ a couple months earlier—without feeling any compunction whatsoever, mind you, to come forward from my position at the back of that small auditorium—I might have been among the legions swarming forth. But despite the intriguing novelty of the phenomenon, the collective energy of so many apparently hungry or curious souls in fluid motion, this present experience didn't have the same appeal as the former event—incidentally, the appeal of physical healing as opposed to spiritual healing are two entirely different things. Even dear Marcella, despite her recent complaints of exhaustion, was adamant that she wanted to go down, and so my friend, receiving her elbow in his, helped her amble the long way there. My own personal conviction was that if the Lord wanted to heal me he could do so the same way he saved me: from right where I was sitting—though he had already apparently passed up the opportunity through the well-intentioned woman who had prayed for me earlier.

This portion of the program—when the charisma and reputation of the big kahuna shines brightest, when like a man on a mission, in a way almost worthy of parody, he begins to march back and forth from one side of the stage to the other to hear the complaints or requests of the restless rabble being allowed one by one to approach him—is when the appeal of such an event becomes most satisfying for those famished for a novel approach to seeking God, a startling and often refreshing change from the typical weekly services they are used to, which are too often defined by banal, predictable routine. For such seekers this kind of gathering can have an intoxicating appeal, with its myopic focus not so much on the proclamation of the traditional gospel message, but more so on the fringe aspects often deemphasized or altogether forsaken in typical church settings, namely the overt demonstration of the gifts and power of the Holy Spirit.

To such eager seekers—that is, those fortunate enough to be allowed on stage—the big kahuna sometimes asks pointed, personal questions. Sometimes he quotes a Bible verse. Sometimes he lays one or both hands on their forehead and shouts, "I rebuke you, devil, in the name of Jesus!" Sometimes he blows a puff of air through the microphone into their face, which sound produces additional dramatic effect, and Boom! they collapse to the stage with an echo, or flail backward uncontrollably like they've been hit with some kind of invisible force. In some cases they are standing all the way across the stage from him, at least twenty feet away, and at his word or even in accord with the mere motion of his arm, their bodies tumble helplessly backward, sometimes into the waiting arms of his dual-purpose assistants. Some lie dead still as though unconscious, others convulse with a full-body shiver, while the big kahuna simply steps around them to attend to the next in line. All of it just as strange as it appears on television. And the truly perplexing thing is that the ones on the receiving end don't seem to be putting on just for show, whether on their own initiative or at the behest of the "ministry" itself, possibly arranged beforehand backstage. Quite the contrary, actually. Something physical, and quite possibly spiritual, appears to be happening to them, but what exactly, and whether for better or for worse, is not entirely clear. And the big kahuna rarely gives much explanation for any of it, with the exception of the vague sort of play-by-play he sometimes offers as he delivers some poor wretch from demons, however real or fictional. At any rate, as soon as the afflicted get back on their feet, some looking as dazed as if they've just been roused from a nap, and either the big kahuna or one of his cronies stick a microphone in their face and bid them explain what the Lord did for them, some of their tearful testimonies seem absolutely genuine and heartfelt, and sometimes you almost feel like crying and clapping for joy right along with them, though in nearly every case whatever sort of healing or deliverance they allegedly received is not readily apparent to the naked eye. And yet for every handful of cases that seem suspicious or implausible, there are always one or two that are not so easy to dismiss without running the risk of rashly passing potentially unjust judgment without knowing for sure one way or the other (especially when the familiar words of Jesus are ringing through your mind: "For with the judgment you pronounce you will be judged, and with the measure you use it will be measured to you"[1]).

But just when the unusual spectacle has your curiosity sufficiently stirred up, and you allow yourself to hope things continue until everyone's needs appear to be met, or even just long enough to help you finally make up your mind as to what the heck is really going on, you are disappointed to hear the big kahuna very casually and subtly bring this portion of the program to a close, which he does with the expertise of one who has done so countless times, glorying in the grandeur of these wonders as he prays his way into another song or two of praise and honor to God—more possible evidence on the side of legitimacy—though this segment hasn't lasted more than forty-five minutes, with maybe a dozen of the multitude given the privilege of being brought on stage. And in the same way that the vast horde of expectant souls only just made their hopeful pilgrimage stage-ward, they are promptly dismissed to their seats.

Eventually my friend returned with Marcella, who was now only further exhausted and doubly disappointed at neither getting on stage nor receiving her healing. In fact, on account of the congested hallways, they hadn't even made it there before being turned back by the returning surge. Just then also, a few seats in front of us, a young couple in their mid-twenties returned, and I was struck by the manner in which the guy in particular plopped down into his seat in a kind of lifeless, defeated way, with neither the expression nor demeanor of one who had had his deepest, or even most superficial, needs met. On the contrary, a single word seemed to summarize him: *disillusioned*.

It wasn't long after this, very probably after receiving a well-intentioned benediction, that we were officially dismissed and began to file slowly back into the bustling hallway, where it suddenly hit me that it was all over already—two hours come and gone like a proverbial blade of grass, a solitary grain of sand slipped through the hourglass. More than that, though it would take the next couple weeks for our conclusions to really sink in and solidify, as my friend and I discussed things on the way home as Marcella slept, or pretended to sleep, and we agreed that most of our initial skepticism remained, it was unsettling to think that our little adventure hadn't helped as much as we had initially hoped. After all, you wouldn't think it should be so complicated. Could something that seemed like a mixture of good and bad really be of God—yes or no? Didn't Jesus himself give pretty straightforward advice along these lines, namely that you will recognize them by their fruits—that grapes are not gathered from thornbushes, nor figs from thistles?[2] If by coming that far all we gained was a better vantage point from which to judge, it was tempting to dismiss the effort as fruitless, though I didn't want to believe that, and still don't. But before most of this sort of thinking even began, just before we reached the elevators, the gist of these sentiments, at that point little more than a mustard seed, was epitomized for me by the almost symbolic sight we encountered there.

On account of our early arrival when we first entered the facility, there had been no real wait to use the elevators, so we got on and off without thinking much about it. But now, with everyone leaving simultaneously, there were crooked lines at least twenty wheelchairs deep in front of both. Not even during my stay at Courage Center for physical rehabilitation a decade earlier had I seen so many wheelchairs so closely gathered, nor have I since. And what struck me so poignantly about the image was not just the fact that so many broken bodies were leaving just as they had come, regardless of what their hopes had been, it was the gloomy looks on most of their faces. To think this "ministry" that touted itself as a worldwide healing crusade on God's behalf was perfectly content to leave so many obvious physical needs—not to mention the not-so-obvious ones—completely unaddressed. Not that I, or probably anyone else, expected all such folks to be healed. My friend and I at least had watched the spectacle enough times over the years to know better than that. Still, if the big kahuna and his planners were truly interested in seeing people healed, why not schedule such events to allow for a couple more hours, if necessary, to at least give each one who comes forward the opportunity to be prayed for, even if nothing outward or profound comes of it? At least then the multitude could be comforted by the knowledge that it was evidently not God's will to bestow such blessings, at least not at that particular time, or for certain individuals. In that case maybe all the sad expressions would have looked less discontented, if only slightly so. At any rate, it made me wonder what Jesus himself would have done if he were there in flesh and blood. I couldn't imagine him just standing there watching these long lines return where they came from unchanged, at least on the outside—this class of individuals who are, more often than not, overlooked and avoided, toward whom Jesus was always particularly compassionate. Yet any avid Bible reader knows that even Jesus didn't heal everyone he came across, though it's equally true that he healed as many as came to him, and no needs—whether paralysis, blindness, deafness, or death— were ever too great or too numerous. Even when he didn't have the time or energy, even when it meant having to put off much-needed rest or his next meal, the needs of others always came before his own—as he put it, "even the Son of Man came not to be served but to serve, and to give his life as a ransom for many."[3]

Sometime later I couldn't help but wonder if this same scenario, this same ugly snapshot, was being repeated at other "crusades" in other cities, even in India, where, as the big kahuna had indicated, the needs were so much greater, thousands upon thousands thronging one another in the presumably oppressive heat of the dusty Indian wilderness, many of them almost certainly without the privilege of wheelchairs or walkers to get there, let alone near the stage. I couldn't help wondering if the man whose hovel I had spotted in that ostensibly godforsaken alley happened to be among the many needy souls swarming around us for the nearest exits, and if so, what would he have thought of the whole production, start to finish—nothing new, just more "Christian" hypocrisy? As for me and my house, I knew better than to blame God for what was clearly not His fault, nor did any of it diminish my faith in Him one solitary jot or tittle, including His ability and willingness to perform signs and wonders at any time and place He may so choose, publicly or privately. I wasn't disappointed that I hadn't been healed because that's not why I had come. Not all disillusionment ends in despair. In fact, the word might even be interpreted positively, as the removal of a kind of veil, allowing you to see things more clearly, even as they actually are, as opposed to what they seem to be. While I sometimes think that receiving or even witnessing a supernatural healing would be great, I learned a long time ago the critical importance of not having your hopes bound up in something so superficial. After all, Judas Iscariot witnessed three years of undeniably authentic, awe-inspiring miracles, and it didn't keep him from the path he chose. There's much more to this passing shadow of a life than being perfectly, or even mostly, physically whole for however long that may last. Though admittedly my status as a profoundly overprivileged American with countless physical, material, and spiritual blessings makes this easier to say than if I were much worse off in one or more of these ways—for example, if I spent my nights beneath an alley-side loading ramp. But again, my personal desire for healing played no part in motivating me to be there. We had come for answers, plain and simple, and though before we reached those pathetic exit lines some nagging questions still festered and would ultimately remain unresolved, I think for the most part I made up my mind right there and then that, even if by the extravagant grace of God there was a sliver of His blessing in some of that to which we had just borne witness, from that point on I would no longer waste any more of my time and energy trying to make sense of this particular man and his so-called ministry.

---

[1] Matt. 7:2

[2] Matt. 7:16

[3] Mark 10:45

State of Mind

I specifically remember remembering not to forget something that I couldn't, and still can't, remember. A memory triggered by the memory of a re-aired NPR *Radiolab* story from 2010[1] that spoiled my leisurely ride home from work several years ago. Spoiled because I was minding my own business and heard too much, more than I bargained for, so that ever since it's been impossible to forget the intriguing segment—or, rather, its implications—as often as I find myself struggling to remember a certain word or phrase or name and can't help but wonder if this is a sign of things to come.

Like many *Radiolab* stories, this one didn't take long to win my attention—in this case my undivided attention, at least at first—beginning, harmlessly enough, with an English professor at the University of Toronto who was taking the novels of Agatha Christie—sixteen of them, written over a span of fifty years—and feeding them into a computer, which rendered the exact number and frequency of words and phrases and their contexts, which, when compared with one another, revealed certain patterns. Having done this previously with Milton's work, the mad professor revealed that this renowned author never used the word *because*. Of what consequence we are left to guess, but there it is. And in the case of dear Agatha, who apparently sold more than a billion books in her lifetime, he noticed that the number of different words she used in her seventy-third novel, which she wrote at eighty-one, had diminished by twenty percent, while her use of indefinite pronouns like *anything, nothing,* and *something* increased six times. This astounded the professor, who published his findings two years after checking them with pathologists, linguists, and statisticians.

In connection with this, the story referenced a "Nun Study" that at the time was still ongoing but has apparently expanded in scope since it was first started at the University of Minnesota, with the goal of examining aging over time. The name of the study stems from the fact that 678 of its participants—who were all over seventy-five when the study began—had at the age of eighteen joined an order called the School Sisters of Notre Dame. These women made ideal subjects not just because of their age and the fact that they led active lives into their eighties and nineties, but because they shared similar backgrounds in various ways, one being that none of them had abused drugs or alcohol. Every year they were given memory tests, and initially these were the only criteria of measure. But one year the study's director was pleasantly surprised to discover that each of these ladies had written an autobiographical essay upon entering the order, and these essays had been preserved.

These papers were then evaluated similarly to the way Agatha Christie's material was, though in this case using the criteria of "idea density" and "grammatical complexity," looking specifically for "the average number of discrete ideas contained in every ten written words." What exactly constituted a "discrete idea" wasn't mentioned. But consider the results. The sisters scoring in the bottom third with regard to idea density were sixty times more likely to develop Alzheimer's than those scoring in the upper third. This finding apparently gave the researchers 92% accuracy in predicting who would eventually develop the disease. And whenever one of these sisters died, a slice of her brain would be taken—which they had all agreed to upon joining the study—and the gurus in their immaculate lab coats would analyze the plaque patterns, lesions, and other relevant minutia and come to their unsettling conclusions.

Yet when the story first aired, the current director warned that this finding was "merely an association" and therefore shouldn't be overemphasized. After all, though Agatha Christie was suspected of having Alzheimer's, she was never actually diagnosed. But the findings are remarkable, and the studies continue, not just in Minnesota but now in multiple places around the country, and almost certainly around the world.

But *remarkable* doesn't adequately convey the power such a simple story can have in turning a routine ride home from work quite grave, contemplative, existential: *The language I used at eighteen has something to do with the state of my mind right now, or thirty years from now?*

This naturally led me to the folder on my bedroom bookshelf containing a few old papers I wrote in middle and high school, one of which includes a series of brief journal entries. Leafing through them, clueless as to what I should be looking for—discrete ideas? grammatical complexity?—I could only wonder: *Are the secrets of my future really lurking in these lines?* If so, there are several digital folders full of further evidence on my computer from my college days, not long after high school—both poetry and prose, fiction and nonfiction, not to mention the trove of e-mails, text messages, and social media posts from the last decade or so. What might *they* reveal?

Not long before turning twenty, I became an inpatient for nine months at a prominent rehabilitation facility in the Twin Cities. I had sustained a severe spinal cord injury the year before, and my first few months there included weekly trips to the on-campus psychologist to assess my state of mind. One day a specialist was brought in to test my cognitive acuity, of which I remember little except that at some point the guy presented a series of words to memorize, and after three or four he asked me to recall them in order. The more I remembered, the more he would add the next time. Then, in the same way, he would ask for the third or fifth or eighth word, until it was clear how many, and which ones, I could recall.

I was surprised how well I did, which the man's facial expressions and mannerisms betrayed as the test progressed. He said he had never seen such a sharp memory, which amused me because I was never among the brightest of my classmates (if such is even any indication thereof). Not only that, I was still a teenager and had only recently learned the particular skill I had utilized on this occasion through a casual coaching session one afternoon from a close friend who happened to be one of the brightest lights in our graduating class. If memory serves, the key to recalling the exact order of several words or ideas was to create a word picture for each. Start by consecutively numbering each one and pairing it with a word that rhymes with that number. Then use that rhyming word as a description for the initial word. If the first word is "photo," it is number one, of course, and you might pair it with the rhyming "ton," envisioning a photograph that weighs a ton. *One ton photo. Two blue elephant. Three free desk.* And so on. Thus you have a vivid image and mnemonic to associate with each word. The irony, however, is that my memory of this may not be as accurate as I might hope. For example, what if you make it to the teens, where everything rhymes the same? At any rate, all I had done was cultivate those pointers now and then in my spare time, challenging myself for fun, which then paid off to some degree, which is to say it temporarily inflated my ego. And if you don't count all the tests I was subjected to throughout my K-12 education, that short session was the first and only time I'd had my memory formally evaluated that way. And whatever the results meant then, I can't help but wonder what, if anything, they may mean for me now, or for the years to come.

But before you get too excited at the prospect of having just learned a clever and novel skill of seemingly limitless value—not least of which being the power to impress and influence everyone you know or encounter—it's worth pointing out what might not be immediately obvious: that using such a method, however effective it may prove in certain settings or for particular purposes, is not how we usually remember things, and is therefore mostly impractical. In fact, its mention here is purely anecdotal. Whether meeting someone for the first time or attending a meeting or reading a book, that method has never been the means I use to store valuable information, nor do I remember using it beyond that single session. Even if it were my preferred technique, I still couldn't help wondering if it would be any more effective than our usual method for storing information long-term. Of course, we don't think of our usual way as a method, since it is much less contrived, and practically automatic, though not quite. Indeed, whether or not we remember a given thing seems to have something to do with how carefully we listen, which essentially comes down to how much we care about that thing, though obviously this is not a hard-and-fast rule, as every well-meaning husband will be quick to point out.

At any rate, a method like the one just mentioned seems like fair evidence that there are, in fact, strategies you can employ to increase the likelihood of retaining memories, both for the short and long term. But for the most part experience seems to teach us otherwise, namely that if you don't use the information you have for various reasons deemed worthy to tuck away in storage, you tend to lose it. But then, as with most everything, there will be exceptions, including much pointless information we never use, like the phone numbers of friends and family from thirty and forty years ago that for some reason still stick with me, or the number pi to fifteen decimal places that I and that same friend mentioned earlier once memorized for the novel thrill of being able to effortlessly recite it on command. Which begs the question why such memories stick around and others disappear. There seem to be a variety of factors that determine this, most of which we are unaware. To give just one example, traumatic memories—whether or not they are suppressed beyond our ability to recall them—seem to stick much more tenaciously than others, despite how much we may wish to be rid of them. The mind obviously has its own peculiar filing and retrieval system that works amazingly well most of the time, which on the one hand seems to operate the same way in all of us, and yet also uniquely from person to person. Needless to say, like the darkest depths of the oceans and universe, so much of the ways and means of the human mind remains, and probably will continue to remain, beyond the reach of our discovery.

More and more these days we hear how vital it is to keep our minds active as we get older, whether through books, crossword puzzles, or sudoku, rather than multiplied hours in front of the boob tube or on Facebook, and I'm sure there's more to that notion than just wishful thinking. Yet in my own case, as I gradually pass from one decade to the next, all my habitual hours of reading, writing, and Scrabble have yet to shield me from the tendency to forget things on an all-too-regular basis. It doesn't matter whether they are things I've known for a long time or things I've just learned, or whether they are important or unimportant. All I know is that I generally remember much better in the morning or afternoon than in the evening, and that nine times out of ten a few short minutes of small talk is all it takes to make me forget the name of someone I've just met. Lately it's also been disconcerting to notice how often I temporarily forget the first or last names of people I know very well, a foul and mysterious "brain fart" that lingers for many minutes or sometimes even hours. Perusing through my high school yearbooks recently for the first time in years, I was appalled at some of the names I had forgotten, first or last, or both. In fact I hardly remembered certain ones even being in our class (I take refuge in the knowledge that there are 165 of them, most of whom I know little more about than their names). I do remember faces, though, even after many years, and in some cases despite substantial metamorphosis of their features, so that should count for something, shouldn't it? But the general trend is not a little disturbing, especially in light of this radio story, though it's easy to keep telling yourself, *You're almost fifty now, what do you expect?* But that doesn't always put your mind at ease, especially when something occurs to you very clearly, and by the time you pull out your phone to look it up or write it down, it's gone. Like it was never there at all. And often no amount of thinking, no matter how intense or well-intentioned, can bring it back. Not all the time, but far too often. Occasionally my eighty-two-year-old mom used to complain of the same, until I would rebuke her with the reminder that forgetting was par for the course at her age, whereas I, more than thirty years younger, am the one shooting double-par, with no valid excuse!

A lot of times the first letter of the word I'm trying to remember floats to the surface of my mind, and it can bob up and down there just beyond my mental reach without another clue offered for many minutes, or even hours. But clinging to solitary letters is not always something you can count on to help you fetch what you are after. I'm reminded of this every time I learn that the letter I think is the first letter of the word I'm trying to think of turns out to be the middle or last letter, which is some help, but not enough. Worse yet, this always seems to happen in front of friends, who waste no time rubbing it in, though I'm quick to point out that I usually do get the letter right, wherever it fits. For example, I recently watched a short video clip involving an actor of substantial fame whose first or last name I absolutely couldn't place, nor could I recall even one of the titles of his many movies, in which he has often played dramatic, villainous roles. But I knew his face like I know my own, and after watching the clip a few more times, the letter *J* kept coming back to me, and I thought that maybe his name was John, though that didn't seem quite right. But it helps to keep repeating it, even if it seems wrong. It seems to tickle the brain's fancy in a way that sends back the vibe that you're on the right track. And wouldn't you know it, the next morning, just after my shower—when many forgotten things suddenly occur to me—Boom, it hit me! James Bader. At least that's what I thought. Then I remembered that he had starred in *Wolf* with Jack Nicholson and Michelle Pfeiffer, which keywords I immediately googled and discovered my error: James *Spader*. But the *J* was spot on.

Another thing I've learned in this regard is that I'm far more likely to recall what seems just barely out of reach if I stop thinking about it so much and just move on to something else. Now and then I might bring the word or key letter back to mind to see if it will break through the surface, but the secret is to let go of it, or at least trick your mind into *thinking* you have (the mind trying to trick the mind?). There is such a fine line between what is hidden and what is evident to our minds. One moment it's irretrievable, and the next it's right there like your first name, like it had been there all along. In this regard a couple lines from conservative historian and teacher Richard Weaver seem pertinent:

> Let us pause long enough to remember that insofar as we are creatures of reflection, we have only the past. The present is a line, without width; the future only a screen

in our minds on which we project combinations of memory.[2]

Imagine being unable to recall something so basic as your address or name or the names or attributes of those you love most, or even the words to complete a single rational thought. Imagine the confusion, frustration, paranoia, and even terror of such an experience, or perhaps the blissful oblivion, the way a newborn sees things. Even for those of us who may never reach that tragic point, the process of remembering sometimes feels like trying to recall the dreams you had the previous night—the mysterious inaccessibility of what only moments before seemed so vivid and tangible and just within reach, which apparent closeness you can almost feel. I've crossed the paths of studies that would likely shed some helpful light on all of this, but their daunting terminology and procedural pedantry alone have dried up any thirst I have for a deeper search along these lines. And yet whether something more than laziness and irritation accounts for this lack of motivation is a fair question, and one which I probably shouldn't be so quick to dismiss. After all, what if such disinterest is just another mechanism of self-preservation, a subtle sign my fragile mind is afraid of learning more along these lines (the mind trying to protect the mind?)?

Those of us blessed with what we might call an active, healthy mind can usually, without much effort, remember scores of first and last times, best and worst times. Times we thought to take another look at how or why or where or when, or who we are or were. Times we thought and thought and thought, and thought we thought. Multitudes of the sounds, voices, and images that we may wish either to remember or forget were burned into our memory banks in ways over which we had, and still have, no say. As mentioned earlier, by virtue of our applied concentration, often through repetition, we possess some degree of power to store away information and remember it. Yet in neither respect is this power absolute. We certainly seem to have no ability to remove, or even distance ourselves from, unwanted memories. When this does happen, it seems to be an involuntary process, which is to say we are not consulted as to whether or not we approve.

I wonder if we can even call *memories* those which we are not able to recall. The answer to that, I suppose, depends on what qualifies them to be called such—our ability to recall them, or simply the fact that they are, or once were, stored in our minds? On the one hand, the momentary or even prolonged inability to recall a given thing doesn't necessarily mean that the idea is no longer in storage. On the other, however clear the notion of those ideas we *think* we remember, the certainty we may feel toward the legitimacy of their existence—including how confident we may feel as far as our ability to retrieve them—is entirely separate from, and therefore almost completely irrelevant to, whether or not they are actually still in storage. After all, what if, at such times, our mind is remembering what was once a memory but has since been forgotten—that is, deleted—or is simply lost somewhere in the brain's equivalent of cyberspace, untethered from anything that might help us remember it? Whether or not the memory is actually there, it is irretrievable. Or maybe our brain is remembering the correct "compartment" in which it was once stored—and therefore we "feel" that inexplicable sensation that we remember something actually in storage—but the memory itself is no longer there. Is it possible to have such a phantom memory, in which case what we remember may be the holding place rather than that which was once held there, the container rather than the content? Like how an amputee sometimes still "feels" an itch or pain corresponding to the empty space where there was once a limb. Or like the thought that opened this essay—the memory of what might or might not have been an actual memory, just the notion thereof, without any particular identity, like remembering you have a Ziploc bag in your pantry but being unable to recall what is in it. Or what if the mind is mistaking the identity of a given idea or experience with another that is similar, which may be stored in the same or a similar or nearby or otherwise contextually related compartment, but the actual memory itself is not there? Whatever the case, all of this reminds me of a memorable quote by former U. S. Defense Secretary Donald Rumsfeld:

> Reports that say that something hasn't happened are always interesting to me, because as we know, there are known knowns; there are things we know we know. We also know there are known unknowns; that is to say we know there are some things we do not know. But there are also unknown unknowns, the ones we don't know we don't know.[3]

At any rate, whether we were active or passive in the making of any of these memories—the ones that actually still exist in storage, that is—they are all equally vulnerable. When you think about it, it's pretty amazing that we started out with something of a blank slate all those years ago, a mostly unleavened lump, and that all that we've accumulated since, for better or worse, the stuff that makes us who we are—objects of each other's love, gratitude, frustration, anger, jealousy, forgiveness, sympathy, and more—is steadily unraveling every day—for some a little, for others more—without apology or permission, and without us really noticing.

And yet forgetting's not all bad. Forgetting has its place as much as remembering. There may be just as much peace of mind gained by forgetting a thing as by the recollection of something else. Just ask anyone with Post-Traumatic Stress Disorder, or with eidetic (i.e. photographic) memory or hyperthymesia (i.e. highly superior autobiographical memory, which unlike eidetic memory is restricted to personal experiences). I remember a television interview not so many years ago revealing with hopeful anticipation the possible release of a new medication which could potentially erase traumatic memories, which by now may be widely available. But the mere thought of what might go wrong with such an allegedly promising treatment seems reason enough to be wary. Just imagine waking one morning with the entire database of your mind wiped absolutely squeaky clean. If we're honest, if there is anything at the top of the list of health-related maladies we fear, it's this. The bulk loss. The total liquidation of everything we have in stock. Going six figures in the red. Whether suddenly or a little at a time—especially before our time.

Imagine for a moment a world like ours, with a similar realm of moon and stars, where no one remembers anything. On the one hand, this makes for a fascinating hypothetical; on the other, can we even call a mind one which can't remember anything? Without hesitation we can say that what we mean by *mind* consists of more than what it can or can't recall—for instance, even in a coma state, the body can't survive without the mind and all of its involuntary directives. But if we're thinking of the conscious mind, no memory means no way to know. No way to move from one thing to the next. To know the cause from its effect. No way to process or believe—only to perceive, if that. No way to contemplate, deliberate, differentiate between love and hate, gladness and sadness, novelty and tragedy. No way to ground or keep around the moment-by-moment happenings of our world, within the sphere of the subjective now, which, when our minds are working properly, they constantly, coherently, exquisitely evaluate to seamlessly translate for us the phenomenal realm of Kant, into a kind of language we can grasp and put to use, for better or for worse. It is this aspect of the mind that confers to us the bulk of our inherent dignity, and yet without it we are no less remarkable beings, or of any less value in the eyes of God—just less as far as our ability to engage with this world into which we were born to thrive.

Whether we are young or old, we glibly joke with family, friends, and strangers about the indignities of aging and losing our minds as though it doesn't bother us a bit, and in truth the greeting card industry wouldn't be the same without such sentiments. We know what could happen at any given moment, but that's the way life always is in so many ways. Besides, this lighthearted bantering is all in fun, because for the most part all is well, and it's good to laugh at ourselves this way, especially since there isn't much else we can do about it. If nothing else, it puts us in our place, reminding us of our human limitations and imperfections, that we're all stuck in the same leaky boat.

This radio story is the kind of thing that can make you paranoid about each word and phrase you ever choose to use, especially in an exercise like this. It makes you wonder if your sentences are dense enough with sense, to protect you, to be the very proof of your apparent mental fitness after all has been expressed just so. And if it hasn't, you're tempted to work through it one more time until it seems as good as you can think to do right now. But then what might *that* indicate, that calculated act of second-guessing, cherry-picking synonyms and clever turns of phrase? Will such a careful process even make a difference as to how our minds wind up in the end? Surely further studies will be needed to investigate the likelihood or otherwise of that. And it's not like we can wait around in the meantime before deciding how to talk or write or, if necessary (God forbid), train ourselves to think. At any rate, you'd like to hope it isn't true that how you thought and wrote when you were young has anything at all to do with who you are today and how you think. You'd like to hope it isn't true that—notwithstanding when, where, how, and by whom you were brought up and educated, in all the ways you've taken mostly for granted through the years—the state of the way you process life and manifest your personality is governed by factors mostly beyond your control.

---

[1] Jad Ubumrad and Robert Krulwich, *Agatha Christie and Nuns Tell a Tale of Alzheimer's*, NPR (Radiolab), Jun. 1, 2010, https://www.npr.org/2010/06/01/127211884/agatha-christie-and-nuns-tell-a-tale-of-alzheimers.

[2] Richard M. Weaver, *Ideas Have Consequences* (University of Chicago Press, Ltd. London, 2013), 158-159.

[3] Donald Rumsfeld, U. S. Secretary of Defense, press briefing, Feb. 12, 2002.

Tell Me Something I Don't Know

I can picture it so easily—the faces and outfits and mannerisms and cheerful chatter—a dozen or more relatives and sometimes family friends, some visiting from out of state, sitting around a dining room table or mingling through the kitchen and living room of whosever house we happened to be in—Thanksgiving, Christmas, Easter, someone's birthday, anniversary, wedding or funeral—the conversations flowing among pairs and trios and at several points as a large group, beginning with the surface stuff: the goodness or badness of the heat or cold or rain or snow, the cattle and corn prices, the latest highlights and heroes of local, college, and pro football, baseball, basketball, golf, not to forget the latest gossip, and how good the food is or was or smells.

Sometimes I think this kind of atmosphere is more than anyone deserves, something more rare and priceless than any of us realize—a loving, caring family that always gets along as often as it comes together, usually at least a few times a year. Never any physical, or even verbal, altercations between anyone, not even once over so many years (my sister and I up until high school graduation don't count; though I can't forget and would be remiss not to mention the multiplied references over the years to the infamous, long-standing feud between Grandma Boetel and her youngest brother, Mark, a spat which allegedly started when the latter criticized the unorthodox ways of a new pastor, which criticism Grandma sharply denounced as unwarranted, which denunciation led to their not speaking to one another for years, which even spread to some of the other siblings; but this was all long before my time). And amazingly all this blissful peace and love and care and fun that we all enjoyed so effortlessly for so long seemed to be almost completely taken for granted by us all—life as usual, as it ought to be, therefore no reason to question or wonder about it one way or another. And this always getting along so swimmingly is the more surprising—and at the same time not so surprising—when you consider the bountiful supply of Old Mil Light and Mogen David at most of these gatherings. And while the morbid side of me sometimes thinks an occasional humdinger of a shouting match or all-out physical brawl would have made for some fun-to-share stories, I'm more than a little glad things turned out the way they did.

But while the mind-blowing privilege of this congenial atmosphere was perfectly wonderful, and more than necessary, it wasn't the only thing we took for granted. Like many other families, I imagine, we also underappreciated something less obvious, which the hindsight of many years has helped make more apparent, at least to me: the rare nature and character of the eldest participants—especially the grandparents, but to a lesser degree also their children, our parents and uncles and aunts—their stoic simplicity and steadfastness, quiet politeness and humility, folksy manners and language—not so much the things they said as how they said them, and how they carried themselves, a threat to no one and a blessing to many. All of which had been shaped and colored by the distinctive hardships characteristic of the era through which they were ordained to pass their most formative years, back when life looked, and also must have sounded, so much different than today—a galaxy away, seemingly—when things were done so much differently, for better and for worse. Days of having to run to the "outhouse" to relieve yourself—without toilet paper, mind you, or at least toilet paper as we know it—whether in blistering heat, driving rain, or bone-chilling winter, even in the pitch-dark night. Days of having your hands pecked by hens each morning as you picked fresh eggs for breakfast, or having your clothes soiled in the process of butchering your lunch and dinner. No washing machines or air conditioning or even electricity or indoor plumbing to ease your efforts, at least in the early post-Depression years, not so very long ago. Though, of course, I'm thinking of rural folks who hardly had two nickels to rub together, which our folks and their folks and undoubtedly their folks' folks also were, the eldest of which being the homesteader pioneers you read about in textbooks, who had everything to lose and little to gain by prospecting in the vacant Midwest prairies, long before government subsidies or crop insurance. A world documented for us by the black-and-white photographs whose plainness seems so fitting to the times that it almost makes you wonder if life itself wasn't in black-and-white back then too. All the unsmiling formality and almost palpable modesty and seriousness so much of the time, even among the children, the more so the further back you go, as if it were taboo to smile or make a funny face, or even pose for the camera the way that I and everyone living after, say, 1950 have taken for granted, almost never without a smile, in accord with the steady evolution and ubiquity of the camera, and the steadily increasing affluence and privileged nature of the rapidly transforming culture—which is to say, in fairness, that they had much less to smile about back then, which by itself highlights the stark contrast between our generation and theirs.

And the more you reflect on the special nature of the superfluous privilege of having had persistent access to this black-and-white generation, the more you're inclined to think that this privilege may in fact have been greater than even the loving atmosphere. This is particularly true because, while this kind of environment could develop in the absence of such individuals, this side-by-side juxtaposition of such divergent generations was not something any of us had the option of choosing for ourselves, which is to say it happened to be our destiny, by the grace and will of God. Whatever the older ones may have thought of this contrast between the austere circumstances they grew up taking for granted and the soft and savory ones their grandchildren were blessed to inherit, together we shared the privilege of bearing witness to this phenomenon. And while for the most part we younger ones missed out on appreciating this contrast at the time for what it was, still it managed to shape our manners and general disposition in a way that could not have happened the same way in other company, however loving and caring. And when you compare this privilege, including all that it has made possible in your life, with the experiences of multitudes less fortunate, past or present, you realize just how fortunate you have been.

And to think how many times these rare characters were gathered together under one roof, often ours, and how altogether oblivious we were to the veritable treasure trove to which we had virtually unrestricted access, lurking just beneath the surface of otherwise polite conversation, stories both ordinary and extraordinary, hilarious and tragic, filled with vivid personalities and ways of life so different from yours you could hardly believe it. Like Dad once mentioning how, when he was a kid, the neighbors would sometimes get their vehicle stuck on the gravel road near their house, and his dad would have to hitch up the horses to pull them out—and this within the same generation that discovered atomic power and the means to put a man on the moon. All of which stories nearly always proved unexpectedly entertaining and enriching, the latter of which you almost never realized at the time. And if the stories themselves are priceless—and believe me, they are—the give and take between each person in the process, full of laughter and frowns and unrehearsed antics, may be more priceless still. In fact these are the kind of conversations and dynamics of company that make you think—not at the time, but years later—more deeply than usual about how flippantly you use a word like *priceless*—if you really mean what you say. Like if someone hypothetically offered you a million dollars in exchange for such memories, would you refuse?

And what do you think could be worse than having taken for granted both these precious souls and opportunities for so long?

The fact that such gatherings don't happen anymore. That's what.

Not in the same way, anyway. For the most part those days are gone forever, never to be repeated. Those particular dynamics between each unique personality at a given place and time and age, interacting in accord with each one's particular relation to one another, the old-fashioned dichotomy in full effect of ladies in the kitchen preparing the meal while the men chit-chat and nibble on appetizers, often in front of the television; and afterward the same schism just as effortlessly kicking into operation, without any complaint whatsoever (unless tongue-in-cheek) from the ones doing most if not all the cleanup. All of which is, of course, simply life at its most usual, which is probably part of why it's so easy to take for granted as it's happening in real time. As if you expect such gatherings of the same personalities, for the same occasions, to continue forever, so that with some of the same people always gathered together in that particular relation to one another, a certain dynamic is enjoyed in a completely unique way. A dynamic you wouldn't change for the world, by the way. Of course, at the time you don't think about a time down the road—closer than you could or would have guessed—when the deaths of the eldest, and the quickly approaching age- and health-related limitations of the next eldest, and the marriages and children and related responsibilities and commitments of the rest—including the need to move away for college or employment or other reasons—will mean the necessary adjustment, and to some degree obliteration, of that treasured Norman Rockwell dynamic in most of its unique facets.

Moreover, these changes come to pass so nonchalantly you hardly notice. Before you are even halfway through high school, Grandpa and Grandma, each after ninety full years, pass away within a year of one another. Perfectly natural, perfectly expected. You shed your tears, or not, ponder for the first time in your life the profundity of Death and all it entails, in particular its permanence. But life keeps you persistently preoccupied as you gather manners and knowledge and practical life experience in general, sprinting through your teens and twenties and thirties fairly oblivious, and since you've never been through it all before you don't sense that anything is amiss as week by month by year by decade the seasons breeze by like weekends. You marry and have kids, or not, and before long the ones you call Auntie and Uncle and Mom and Dad, who were always so active and independent with their work and golf and garden and travel—paying the bills, fixing the meals, and keeping the household machine well-oiled in general—begin very gradually, very subtly, to slow down, starting with retirement. Perfectly natural, perfectly expected. Life falls into different patterns of routine, the gatherings continuing, maybe a couple less per year than before, and a slightly different dynamic every year if you are sharp enough to notice, though mostly you do not. Then Grandpa Stamp passes, and pretty soon Granny Schade and Aunt Jerry and Uncle Maurice. Then even old Jerry Micheel, who was like family and seemed like he would always be around, like Andy Griffith. And right about the time you start noticing, which inevitably triggers the thought of who's next and what that means, Aunt Norma slips away, and a year later

Uncle Bob—half of Mom's siblings gone, just like that. The following year it's Uncle Bryce, older than any of them—the end of an era, in the words of his wife—followed eight months later by her best friend and brother, our own dearly-beloved dad, and, just five months after that, our dearly-beloved mom. And every time this happens, even when the writing has been on the wall for many weeks or months beforehand, you're still blown away by how quickly so many who were so precious to you can disappear from the scene like a wisp of smoke, leaving an ominous void that is felt the more when, less than three weeks later, the call comes about Aunt Gloria, and less than a month after that, Mom's twin brother and last remaining sibling, my uncle Lyle.

Needless to say, such a rapid succession of departures among those you knew and loved most—the last eight of them in just four years—leaves you with plenty to contemplate, including the reality that those who remain from the black-and-white era can now be counted on one hand. And as for the prospect of gathering together, if only for the memorial services, the personas in possession of the choicest perspectives and stories are not just fewer now, but less able than ever, because of distance and fragile health, to gather, or be gathered, or even to remember. I don't so much mean the localized gatherings of family within fairly close proximity to one another, which in some cases continue, but especially the gatherings that used to happen occasionally for holidays or other special events, when you might see some of the distant ones from other states you haven't seen in several years. And this is the more lamentable because in some sense these eldest ones made the gatherings what they were for so long, what no subsequent get-togethers will be without them. And when the accumulated bulk of the implications of all this lands on you as if without warning, blunt as a tombstone, all you can do about it is sit there with your mouth open, shaking your head and scolding yourself to stop taking so blasted much for granted.

I can recall a number of return rides home after one of these beloved gatherings, savoring, with teary eyes, the incomparable blessings of it all. Not just the usual amiable atmosphere and dynamic, but the much rarer treasure of specific details gained through the unexpected telling of one or more colorful stories of life as it once was and never will be again. At the same time, I can't forget other return rides when, after having experienced the usual blessings, the bliss was substantially diminished by the realization that no such priceless stories had been told, at least none that yielded any unforgettable gems. Which made me think I should have intervened with some questions or comments that could have possibly opened the door. But since I had missed my chance, the only thing to do, besides regret it, which changes nothing, was to resolve never to make such a careless mistake again. I even imagined inaugurating a new tradition at the next gathering, where, just before or after dinner, story time could be stimulated by the following simple suggestion: *Tell me something I don't know* (about the old black-and-white days, I would explain). After all, with so many representatives of the black-and-white generation together in the same house, why squander even one opportunity?

And while I remember this new idea crossing my mind more than once while sitting down to dinner at subsequent gatherings, it seemed not just quirky to make such a suggestion, but contrived, as people were already engaged in spontaneous conversation as usual, which is part of what made the gatherings and the particular dynamics thereof what they were, so why try to force a square peg through a round hole? Besides, isn't it true that good things come to those who wait? Anyway, all it takes is some little detail, just the right one, to trigger a tangent or someone's memory, and just like that the magic happens in its own proper time and manner. The preceding conversation might be so mundane as to have you yawning for a change of subject, when suddenly, amid the background chatter, a new and potentially intriguing topic emerges, instantly piquing your interest, and sometimes also everyone else's.

Like when someone mentions the time Uncle Bob set the chickens on fire, or the other time he threw one or more of the cats down the well—each of which is like the tip of an iceberg, with a whole world of further details hidden beneath. Or when Grandma's mother chased Aunt Norma through the house with a large knife (and here we thought *Grandma* was formidable). At least that was always her contention whenever the subject happened to come up—and as a matter of fact it seemed to be brought up almost every time the four siblings got together. "Oh, Norma, she did nothing of the sort," one of them would inevitably provoke her, to which she would predictably retort, "She most certainly did! I should know, I was there!" (Incidentally, when I asked Mom about whether I remember this rightly, she said no, *she* was the one who got chased with the knife, and that in fact Norma was always the favored "pet" of this ornery battleax who was further described as "mean, mean, mean," who also allegedly threatened to cut off her fingers for the unthinkable crime of biting her nails.) Or the time when these same siblings together wondered what ever happened to Grandma's amputated leg after she died, which apparently had been kept frozen up until then. Round and round they went, each venturing its fate, which the next would just as strenuously deny, offering their own reasons why such couldn't possibly be the case, and why their own hypothesis was much more plausible. Yet even more precious than the actual answer, however lost to history it may now be—Mom claims it was slipped into the casket of some unwitting John or Jane Doe just before burial—is the surviving memory of their playful rapport. Maybe even better than the hearty laughs we all enjoyed at the time, including whatever little comments or questions we each might have thrown in with the hope of fanning the flames. Which is to say nothing of the potential value of the opportunities that still remain (for those of us who remember) to share these stories. And not just with the younger generations of relatives, but with friends, acquaintances, even strangers.

Good-old times like these make me wonder what the gatherings were like when the grandpas and grandmas themselves were kids and young adults, both before and after they were married, before and after they became parents. Were some of the conversations in German, or some less-civilized breed of English? Did they allow themselves the luxury of laughter during hard times, or at least less prosperous ones than ours? Were their traditions different? Did they, too, pray before each meal? What kind of stories did *their* parents and grandparents tell? Tearjerkers about their respective motherlands, full of famine and fear and beloved relatives left behind, never to be seen or perhaps even heard from again? Or maybe breathtaking, sometimes first-hand accounts of the harrowing voyage across the Atlantic in a primitive steamship, or from the East Coast to the Midwest by horseback and covered wagon? Those must have been some impressive and unforgettable stories, though sadly none were ever passed down like an heirloom to any of us by way of oral or written tradition.

Speaking of heirlooms, up until recently a massive antique trunk of unknown origins had been sitting for years in my parents' basement, the kind those hardy ancestors of ours would have lugged around on their arduous journeys. It had the most wonderful musty smell inside that I always loved when we opened it every year to get out our Christmas decorations. Yet as long as this old relic sat there in plain sight being persistently ignored and unappreciated by otherwise preoccupied souls, a kind of forgotten symbol of former times, it never once struck me, until it was recently given away, how lamentable it is that such things have no voice to share their own priceless stories.

But as much as the perspectives and stories of the black-and-white generation are precious and irreplaceable and will be greatly missed, it's not like those of us who remain can no longer enjoy gathering once they are all gone. The only question is, will we?

As already mentioned, as far as I am aware, for the most part the only family gatherings happening among those with whom my family and I keep in contact are fairly localized, within immediate nuclear family circles, mostly parents and their kids and grand-kids, gatherings which still happen anywhere from a couple to a few times a year on both sides of the family. Though several of us extended relatives do keep in fairly close touch by some combination of email, telephone, and social media, by and large we have been seeing less and less of one another in person for years now. This shouldn't be surprising, but our tendency to take these routines and traditions for granted deceives us into complacency in this regard. The distance between us, more than anything, hinders or prevents our gathering, though it's always been this way with the cousins and aunts and uncles from out of state. Seeing some of them even once every several years has always been a special treat, and about as good as we can hope for given the substantial distance between us and the busyness of life in general. This is something we have always just accepted and taken for granted. If we have complained about it, we have only done so in a senti-mental sort of way when expressing to one another how long it's been since the last time, and how nice it is to actually be together again.

Beyond the bare fact of reducing the likelihood of getting to-gether, this distance factor has another unfortunate downside: our relationships with those far away generally tend to be less in-timate, if we have them at all. Of course, this all depends on how often and by what means we stay in touch. In the case of some of my cousins, second cousins, aunts, and uncles, we hardly know one another because we have spent little, if any, time together, es-pecially in person. Even if some of us talk by phone, it might only be once or twice a year, if that, and likewise through the mail, usu-ally just a birthday or anniversary or Christmas card, the latter sometimes containing a family photo and form letter summary of what's been happening recently. Some of us second cousins have never even met or communicated with one another in any way, and maybe never will, even in this enlightened era of ubiquitous internet, smartphone, and social media. And even if a connection is made, including via video-call, while it is certainly a step up from a typical phone call, as far as intimacy, it's still not the same as interacting with one another face-to-face—enjoying a meal and various activities together, breathing the same air, saying our hel-los and goodbyes with hearty hugs and kisses. No matter how so-phisticated technology gets, even in so-called virtual reality, ava-tars and emojis will never be a satisfactory substitute for the real thing.

Naturally, you can't help but wonder how different your lives and relationships with these folks might be if only you had been born and raised within closer proximity to one another, or for whatever reasons deliberately chose to relocate in order to live closer together. This, of course, would have completely changed the dynamics of most, if not all, of the gatherings you grew up taking for granted, and might still be taking for granted, allowing the potential to get together more often, and for closer ties to be formed. As a result of those very different interactions from what would have been if you couldn't gather as regularly due to distance, you would all be substantially different personalities. But again, since we almost universally recognize this opportunity only in hindsight, often after already having established ourselves at a given job in a certain town where the kids are in school and making friends and it seems like as good a place as any to settle down, we tend to miss out on the opportunity to move wherever we like so as to foster closer relationships with the people we love most, provided a person has the means and desire to do so. But obviously tearing up whatever roots you presumably worked hard to establish, without any promise that relocating will make life better, is something of a gamble with unknown implications for the future. At any rate, it's amazing how close some of us cousins and aunts and uncles are despite the distance that separates us and how little time we have spent together through the years, even through correspondence, and in some cases despite how little we have in common. But for the most part this closeness some of us enjoy is the result of having been connected early in our upbringing more than with other relatives, especially in person, which established a link, and in some cases a bond, that distance and a general lack of intimacy with one another have not yet been able to sever.

This reminds me of how excited everyone always was all those years ago whenever we separated ones got together after a long time apart. It didn't seem to matter whether it was with the ones with whom we kept in closer touch or those we almost never saw or heard from. In spite of whatever distance and lack of communication separated us, the flesh-and-blood tie held fast. Just being together seemed to be enough—eating, drinking, laughing, and reminiscing about old times (the adults, that is, as we kids scampered about, mostly oblivious, until we were old enough to appreciate it a little more, though still deficiently). All of which makes me wonder how often, and for what reasons, American families both nuclear and extended get together these days. Are people more inclined, or less, to gather now than in previous decades? And whatever the composition of these gatherings, regardless of the occasions, is it more common or less for those who gather to get along? Regardless of the answers to these, one thing about these gatherings is undeniably certain: as in my own family, the representation of the black-and-white generation is quickly becoming extinct. Which is to say we are all missing out on something unique and rare, which will never again be experienced by any families in quite the same way.

On another note, whatever the particular dynamics may be within these families, it should also be mentioned that all this technology that enables those of us who are physically separated to keep in touch more intimately (via video calls) and constantly (i.e. from anywhere at any time, via cell phone) can at the same time prove to be a hindrance to direct interaction and intimacy as often as we do happen to get together. That is, it should go without saying that the degree to which we are preoccupied with these devices when we do gather in person will ultimately determine the trajectory and outcome of the gatherings, including the nature of our relationships with one another.

On the one hand, you could say that the future is wide open with opportunity for us younger ones related by blood and genetics to gather as often as we are able and willing, whatever the occasion. At the very least we have no excuse, technology-wise, not to keep in touch. It's simpler now than it's ever been. At the same time, it's not easy to reach out and make contact with relatives you

hardly know in order to kindle, or rekindle, the dry coals or smol-
dering embers that are the solitary tie that binds you. Beyond the
initiative necessary to do so, it's worth considering your motive.
If all you have in common with these folks is the same family tree,
you wouldn't be blamed for wondering if this is reason enough for
trying to establish a closer connection. The thought of trying to
start from scratch in this regard seems about as awkward as going
on a blind date. What could be more uncomfortable than sitting
around a table with one or more strangers—relatives, no less—
not quite knowing what to say to one another? In contrast with
the old-time gatherings, it is colossally disheartening to imagine.
Even if we did get together now and then, whatever stories we
might share with one another would almost certainly pale in comparison with those told by the black-and-white generation. At
least that's my reflex thinking. In that sense those old gatherings
spoiled those of us who were privileged to be a part of them. Of
course, that's not the best reason to persuade yourself out of the
possibility of making such efforts, but when you're already disin-
clined to the idea, even such a flimsy excuse will suffice.

Thinking of just the cousins and second cousins, we do have
in common the general affluence and technological progress that
has come to define the era in which we all grew up and now sub-
sist, which has left its indelible mark on each of us in a similar way,
just as the austere circumstances faced by the black-and-white
generation made its mark on them so much differently. In our
case, this common ground includes certain shared tastes in various aspects of popular culture like sports, news, music, movies,
and social media, which means there isn't a wide enough gap in
our experiences that the older could much impress the younger
with tales from our youth. There isn't the sharp contrast there always was between the experiences of the spoiled-rotten generation of us post-World War II, post-Vietnam kids and those

diehards of the Depression era, which is almost like comparing life on earth with life on the moon. Maybe it's true the younger ones would be entertained by hearing us older ones explain what life was like when we were their age, the television a sizable piece of furniture with a single knob, less than ten channels, and no remote control, and that we somehow managed to survive without smartphones, having endured the inhumane indignity of searching for answers in actual rather than virtual books and libraries. Yet I wonder how much mileage we could really squeeze out of such conversations. So when it comes down to it you have to ask yourself: Are there other reasons beyond our common DNA that justify going to the effort of beginning, and then maintaining, a new relationship, and possibly even getting together now and then?

But this is such pitiful, glass-half-empty thinking, practical though it may seem. On the other, more optimistic hand, it is remarkably sad to think of relatives who are still able and healthy enough to gather ceasing to do so, or even just to keep in touch, which doesn't really require that much of us, does it, however busy we claim to be? The more hopeful side of me wants to believe that those of us who experienced the old-time gatherings could actually find common ground with some of these relative strangers by sharing some of the gems we remember best, since they may not have been as privileged to enjoy such, nor may have even heard any of the same or similar stories from their own parents or grandparents. But then I haven't been part of whatever gatherings have been taking place over on their side with the parents and grandparents and siblings of the spouses of my cousins, which is to say I am equally ignorant of the stories they have also surely been telling for decades now. And who knows, maybe by sharing with one another our mutually unique experiences we might intrigue or impress one another or induce each other to fits of laughter or tears. That's the wonderful thing about telling such stories and hearing them told, especially when there are multiple people included—you never know what they may yield. The stories themselves don't necessarily need to be thrilling. In fact, some of the most interesting and powerful are actually the most ordinary, and since when is ordinary a bad thing?

But beyond enjoying the blessing of pleasant company in a loving atmosphere, as well as being able to carry on the tradition of family gatherings with the next generation, including whatever stories these gatherings make possible in the process, now and then one of these simple stories blindsides you with such force that you are left beside yourself with wonder.

Like the one I got the surprise privilege to hear more than a decade ago—by a perfect stroke of providence, a sudden, serendipitous change in conversation—about the little blue Volkswagen Beetle I had often heard that my dear mom once drove, which once upon a time rolled over in a snow-packed ditch outside of Sioux Falls one dark and dreary evening, years before I was even thought of. A story, it should be noted, that was told so matter-of-factly that its irony only landed on me long after the telling was over. And the fact that nearly everyone in the room but me was familiar with the story made me wonder why I'd been left out of the loop for so long, and how many other such stories I might be ignorant of.

Never mind what caused the little Bug to fly off the road, whether sheer ice, as Mom claimed, or one beer too many, as someone (my guess is Uncle Bob) wasted no time suggesting with a snicker that caught on. Despite the somber details—that it was Christmas Eve or Christmas Day around ten p.m., and she was on her way to Huron for a bowling tournament but had been thrown from the vehicle and was apparently wandering in vain in search of her shoes—the room was full of smirks and giggles, since they all knew the story ended well, which almost sounded like an old joke you've heard too many times, including a passing car that soon stopped to give the poor gal a ride.

"The guy was drunk as a skunk," she explained, though apparently she hadn't noticed until she was already in and on the way—not that she could be too picky just then about who was driving. At any rate, it wasn't long before they happened upon a small town, which of course had a small bar, and so, shoeless and probably shivering cold, she proceeded inside to use the phone.

"I don't remember *who* I called," she replied, looking sincerely sheepish and perplexed in response to the first of several questions.

Without missing a beat someone claimed *she* was the person called, then someone else agreed, while another disagreed, as the details, fictional or otherwise, enumerated. After a couple minutes of this, the one voice that hadn't yet made a peep suddenly piped up with his typical, almost-straight-faced sarcasm, as he answered his own question—"Who do you *think* she called?"—by pointing his thumb at his chest. And now that he had everyone's attention, he added that he was *always* the one getting called in situations like this—more evidence that this wasn't the only such story I hadn't heard—before they were even married, mind you, and he was milking it for all it was worth as though there were something to be gained by it. Which, of course, all of us who knew and loved him fondly remember as his unique and funny way of taking the entertainment value of a story to the next level through subtle, deliberate, seemingly innate exaggeration, which enabled us all to savor it the more, so that pretty soon the cackles really started letting loose, and more details and disagreements—and if we were fortunate that afternoon, another related tangent, even if it didn't involve anyone present or part of the family.

And despite how content I was just being there, soaking it all in—a profound gift worth more than any compliment or award I've ever received—I was also struck dumb. Because as entertaining as it was to hear the story told that way with the lively help of loved ones who each seemed to enjoy this collective ride down memory lane, and as compelling as some of the extraneous details were—like when its central characters returned to the crash site before leaving town that evening to retrieve the Christmas gifts strewn about the ditch and field, they arrived just in time to chase away a greedy pair of opportunists caught red-handed trying to plunder the scene; or when they returned the following day to tow away the wreck and Dad happened to spot something glistening in the field beyond, and it turned out to be Mom's glasses—it wasn't either of these details that I was left thinking about. Rather, beyond any of the specifics of the story or the antics of those who told it, what seemed the more profound takeaway was what such a seemingly insignificant story can mean in the grand scheme of things for a person in my position, hearing such things for the first time—namely that, had things happened just a little differently in even that one situation, I might not be around to hear about it, or to ponder its implications, including the ability to enjoy the innumerable experiences my simple life has been afforded, among them the opportunity to ask myself so many years afterward: *What if I had never heard it?* Which would change none of the facts, only my contemplation and appreciation of them, and for the incomprehensible wisdom and sovereignty of the true and living God.

It's stories like this that have the unexpected power to take you completely by surprise, to shake and shape your perspective from that point forward. Like the one about Dad falling down the stairs as a toddler and hitting his head against the cistern so hard that he permanently lost hearing in one ear—an instant life-changer in countless ways that he would from that moment begin to discover. Had he struck that concrete slab any harder, my sister and I might not be around. Just think how many game-changer moments like that have happened in the lives of each of your parents, siblings, spouse, and children, as well as your own. Just imagine the stories, the multitudes of details, of which both you and they are presently ignorant with regard to one another. If only something had happened the slightest bit differently in any of them, just imagine the potential implications. And just think how quickly that blissful ignorance of yours or theirs could change one day when you least expect it—not to mention the implications thereof, for better or for worse—through the simple telling of one seemingly ordinary story.

Death Talk

So Mom and Dad sat me down and had The Death Talk, my sister tells me with a telltale smirk, about fifteen years ago.

It was a conversation we had never had together, though we would discover it was the first of many more to come, both between the two of us and also with them. That is, now that we were all apparently old enough—Sarah and I in particular, having graduated the happy-go-lucky days of our teens, twenties, and some of our thirties in route to the unthinkable threshold separating what we still consider the vibrant flower of our youth from the austere no man's land of post-fifty-hood.

Their initial talk began simple enough, the three of them casually chitchatting around the kitchen table at breakfast or lunch, until the expressions of Ma and Pa suddenly turned somber. Shortly after which Sarah found herself on a guided tour from room to room and floor to floor in a way she never had before, receiving specific instructions about the house and life insurance, which photos and furniture, jewelry and knickknacks and keepsakes and crystal-ware, ranked in terms of importance and which did not. Which should be auctioned and which should be given, or not given, away, and to whom, and why or why not. Except for their vehicles, I don't think the contents of the garage or backyard shed were included, but they still covered a good deal of ground for a first conversation on the topic, down to the detailed plans they had already ironed out with both their lawyer and mortician, including which hymns they each wanted sung, and which Scriptures read.

When their appointed time arrived.

That's what all this was about. What they couldn't seem to help talking about in anything but solemn tones, at least in breaching the subject. A conversation which for so many years had been conveniently avoided, mentioned in passing, if at all, sometimes with a laugh among relatives and friends—*after we are long gone, ha ha ha*—and on to the next subject. After all, what use was there addressing these things back when we were just pea-brained college kids without a care in the world, and they too were just as healthy and hunky-dory, just as independently enjoying active lifestyles as we were—not one of us thinking more than a moment longer than necessary about the potential nearness of our demise? Purposely discussing the inevitable loss of one another? Are you kidding? What fun would that have been? Including the related, necessary burden of thinking through what to do with all the stuff that's left behind, valuable or otherwise. Why not rather cross that precarious bridge somewhere down the road? That's the perpetual temptation and tendency, the reassuring little voice that allows you to put it off another day and week and month and year, convinced you'll get around to it eventually—someday. Besides, there are always more preferable things to talk about, namely what's going on in the here and now, so why block out the warm, bright sunshine of such pleasantries with the dark and dreary thunderheads of Death Talk?

That gloomy phrase inadvertently coined by my sister that we've both found funny ever since. Every time the subject would come up and with a giggle we'd speak it aloud, sometimes in deep, pseudo-menacing voices. Dwelling on Death and all it entails, if only briefly. The idea of it. The formality and novelty. Otherwise unwitting young adults finding themselves forced to confront the issue head-on, ready or not, in a way they have never had to, an experience about as eye-opening and surreal (I would imagine) as signing your marriage license or witnessing the birth of your first child. At any rate, a landmark event, a kind of rite of passage that awakens you afresh to the fact that, if it hasn't sunk in yet, regardless of how young you feel, you belong to the adult world. Not that you're unaware of this, but sometimes you need a whiff of the smelling salts every now and then to arouse your attention afresh.

Of course, we twenty-first-century Americans have no lack of distractions to keep us from thinking too long about any serious subject like this. And as already noted, it's no secret or newsflash that we'll naturally be prone to avoid this one in particular. But on top of that, when you happen to be a young adult who hasn't yet had a mortgage or marriage or child of your own, when you haven't yet had to bury a parent or sibling or spouse or child, though you are no less an adult and are not without the experience of having tasted something of the painful aftermath created by the deaths of others for whom you are not responsible for carrying out their final wishes, it's not surprising that the novelty of this new responsibility catches you off guard at first. In fact, it strikes you funny, in the sense that you suddenly find yourself in this unique position, which you had for so long taken for granted as belonging to those more mature, experienced, and trustworthy, who both looked and acted the part, bona fide adults without question, who were responsible for everything else, always somehow seeming to possess an innate knowledge of exactly what needed to be done in any given situation. Had they and their siblings had the same sorts of conversations with their parents at an earlier age, including the little household tours? At any rate, it's not like you have the presence of mind as a kid to ask pertinent questions along the way that might one day help you act with similar prudence. Which means that it's only much later that you realize, with some alarm, that you've already arrived at that place you never thought much about most of your life, where the spotlight has suddenly shifted and you're no longer watching the game aloof from the safe distance of the bleachers or dugout, or even just taking practice swings in the on-deck circle. You're in the batter's box, digging in, and the team is counting on you.

However, as often as my sister came to visit and we discussed these guided tours with further instructions that continued, I found myself wondering why I seemed to be getting left out of the loop, since I was always learning of these planning sessions afterwards, when my sister would describe the latest developments. At first it hurt my pride, but a moment's reflection was all it took to reveal what hadn't occurred to me initially, namely the blatantly obvious reality that when the dreaded days would inevitably come—which they now have—when whole rooms and closets, drawers and shelves, cupboards and crawlspaces, need to be accessed and cleaned out, and boxes and vehicles packed, some of which requires the ascending and descending of staircases, how is the one in the wheelchair with oven mitts for hands and the strength of a third-grader supposed to contribute, aside from giving orders?

And while these candid conversations between my sister and me always retained some degree of levity—as do nearly all our conversations—eventually certain potentialities and probabilities have to be considered and addressed. Like whether nursing home, assisted living, home-health care, or hospice care is the most appropriate option at each of several stages, including the financial implications of each. However, in terms of planning, there's only so much you can do beforehand to be prudent and proactive about such things, doing your small part so that when the time inevitably comes that you are bent double with tears and all-too-vivid memories, however positive, there is that much less to have to think through and decide on the spot, thereby relieving you of any additional emotional stress. And in our case this experience was eased the more because the ones for whom we were planning, who spent their entire adult lives, often at great personal sacrifice, even to the very end, going out of their way to help make our lives as pleasant and carefree as humanly possible, had already made most of the important decisions.

Another beneficial service these tremendous role models unwittingly bequeathed to us kids is consistently having lived the example of not living for things, including money—that is, the love of it and all it has the power to procure, and corrupt. Over the course of a decade or so of increasingly frequent Death Talks with us, neither of them seemed to care much at all about the things they stood to leave behind, materially speaking. Understandably, as her own final days crept quietly closer, Mom did occasionally express some reluctance about parting with certain household items for such cheap prices as my sister worked hard to clean out the house, but in the end she acquiesced with a peaceful heart and mind, recognizing the practical need to get rid of them over the reasonable desire to get a fair price for things she knew were worth much more, even if only sentimentally. This attitude of being able to so easily let go of the things they spent a lifetime accumulating was probably largely the result of each of them having been raised during the post-Depression 1930s and 40s on South Dakota farms, each knowing almost nothing of excess or privilege—unless by *excess* you mean hard work and strife, and by *privilege* you mean just enough food to get by day by day, and a change or two, at most, of clothing for each family member. Consequently, even before meeting and having kids, they each began their adult lives with little more than a car apiece and perhaps the hope of a slightly better life than what they had known. But more than that, this attitude was shaped and put into proper perspective by the common faith they shared in the God of the Bible, the incomparable riches of whose promised eternal inheritance—through the priceless gift of the forgiveness of sins for those who put their trust in Jesus Christ—makes it so much easier to leave behind all lesser things, including flesh and blood.

Yet despite having grown up in a much more affluent and privileged era than they did, my sister and I have been thankful to discover that this same practical disposition of detachment in regard to money and things has evidently rubbed off on us. Anything we stood to inherit has meant next to nothing to either of us, aside from a few household items that we will treasure keeping around to remind us of these precious ones we have lost. Even if it did come down to the need to divide the spoil, I'm certain that we would each far sooner forsake our own share in favor of the other than ruin our relationship over it. Life is far too short for such nonsense. Which makes it doubly sad and hard to fathom how so many siblings, widows, and extended relatives are driven at one another's throats or even into the courtroom over such. And why? For the sake of mere *things* or filthy lucre they too will soon have to part with likewise?

In fact, if we would but stop for a minute to think about it, the irony of this prospect becomes clearer than usual, or at least it should. As it is, we are too often altogether oblivious to this reality—two obvious realities, really, hiding in plain sight—which we all realize but seldom acknowledge. First, the fact that it's all just stuff, so much clutter, almost junk, in some sense practically without any value whatsoever. The things by which or on which or in which we so often sit and walk and sleep and dress and eat and play and laugh and speak without caring one whit about most of the time. Until, that is, the rare days we are confronted with the thought of losing some or all of it, having known the whole time, deep down, that this is inevitable. And in this light it's actually surprising that the very dust that so constantly settles upon it all isn't a more frequent reminder to us that that's all any of it really is.

However, in another sense just as real as the first, it's also equally plain to recognize that all of this is not just stuff, nor junk. Nearly every item, however meaningless or meaningful to us, has its own story. How it was purchased or found or received as a gift. The fancy fortune of birthdays, holidays, anniversaries, weddings, vacations, garage sales, inheritance, etc. How much or how little time and hard work we had to endure in exchange for the item. Each piece, however valuable or invaluable money-wise or senti-mentally, has its place among the household, and together the whole of it comprises a unique kind of portrait or fingerprint or soul of a household that defines a little something of who we are, both as individuals and as a family unit. Consider how each room can have its own particular theme or character, down to the colors and design scheme of the carpet, bedding, drapes, and walls, as well as what hangs on them and decorates the shelves. Clean it all out and what's left? The lackluster void with which you started back in the beginning, before any of these things had accumulated, before they were so specifically arranged, and thereby given added meaning, when both your individual and family portrait looked so much different, vacant of personality—the difference between a house and a home.

And while parting from our loved ones is usually more diffi-cult and painful for most of us than letting go of all things material, it still isn't always easy. This final letting go of things tends to be particularly hard for those without any hope of life beyond the grave—if this life is truly all there is. In that case it's no wonder some feel cheated, bitter, full of regret and resentment, often at the God they allegedly don't believe in and have long wanted noth-ing to do with, except when it comes to looking for someone to blame. After all, they've exchanged so much time and effort for everything they have, materially speaking. And yet no matter how easy or hard it is for a person to let go, either way it can be depressing to ponder the sort of depreciation that happens the instant you realize how little value things actually have in the grand scheme of things once there is no longer anyone left to appreciate them. No matter what they may have cost in dollars or Deutschmarks. No matter how much they once meant to you, or how many generations they have been passed down in the family, even the meaning and essential worth of such beloved things can be reduced to little more than nothing depending on who stands to inherit them. In this case, as in love, the old adage proves true: *Beauty is in the eye of the beholder.* Sad as it is to contemplate, everything eventually depreciates this way. Because in the final analysis, as the Bible has testified all along, it all came from dust, and to dust it shall all return.

Like it or not, this is what it all inevitably boils down to: however closely attached you are to any of it, it must all be let go of. Although this is really a passive way of putting it, which removes some of the sting by excluding the personal aspect. Stated more directly: *we* must let go of it all, each and every one of us. However precious any of it is to us, we must be prepared to kiss it goodbye forever. And this is among the simplest of the questions we have to face in this regard.

This idea of needing to let go reminds me of something I heard once about coffins that have drawers in them (no joke), presumably for the purpose of bringing things along for the "journey" like they apparently used to do for the mummified pharaohs in their pyramids. If this doesn't demonstrate how much some cherish their earthly treasures, I don't know what does. Or consider something I once learned from someone who would know about the burial chambers in a local mausoleum being priced in accord with their physical altitude. That is, they are stacked one upon another, and the higher the chamber—and therefore, in the words of this source, "the closer to heaven"—the more expensive. Both of which examples seem funny at first, until you realize that many people are dead serious about these things (pun intended).

In any case, it goes without saying that all this thinking and talking and planning for such things is a whole other thing entirely from actually having to carry it all out—which is like the difference between talking about and actually running a marathon. To go through the exhausting motions of sifting through and distributing the remnant of your loved one's shoes and sweaters and dishes and knickknacks to every available, willing relative, friend, acquaintance, or stranger, or, as a last resort, to the local thrift shop or auction. The very thought of this makes you cringe and want to change the subject, but unless you plan to burn it all, it has to go somewhere. And while it can be somewhat cathartic to handle each of these things up close in the process of dismantling the unique personalities of each and every room and floor, which inevitably triggers multiplied memories, positive or negative, this process almost invariably makes more poignant your sense of pain and loss. Moreover, it's more than a little disconcerting to discover what a pathetic pittance certain items bring from those who are doing you the great service of taking them off your hands, no matter how beautiful or valuable or deeply invested with sentimental worth.

Of course, there are always non-negotiables, like Mom and Dad's wedding rings, or the "family Bible" with the handwritten listing in the front recording where and when the grandmothers and grandfathers on Dad's side were born and died, which stretches back as far as 1828, from England and Germany to Pennsylvania, Iowa, and South Dakota. But so many other things fall into a kind of intermediate category, like the gorgeous grandfather clock Dad bought after Grandpa Stamp passed, or the scores of one-of-a-kind black-and-white photos—surely these dare not be left to just anyone? But then you have to draw the line somewhere, since you can only keep so much—especially in my case, in a one-bedroom apartment, and Sarah living overseas. And of course no matter who takes any of it, every last thing will eventually have to be left behind again, and then where, or to whom, will it all go? Will a local museum even want black-and-white photos of people they don't know, without any significance beyond their novelty? And what about all the in-color pictures? Since neither Sarah nor I have our own children to leave them with, will even close friends or relatives, or their children, want any of these? The question is hardly worth asking, though it won't be long before there won't *be* any more black-and-white photos for anyone to worry about, nor even perhaps any physical pictures whatsoever, since they are all quickly becoming digitalized, which seems greatly to diminish their nostalgic value, no matter how many manage to survive (even the multitudes that do survive tend to be haphazardly stored in a series of folders on our phones or computers and often backed up "in the Cloud," the vast majority of which are never organized, let alone looked at; in this way just imagine how the personal and collective histories of entire societies could be instantly obliterated by a single digital blitzkrieg in the form of an electromagnetic pulse or some other similar catastrophe). In the case of our family, the nostalgic value of the remaining non-digital photos is heightened the more because there are more than a dozen albums full, each arranged in a particular order, often with handwritten notes beneath or on the back, each telling a multi-generational, often chronological story of families and friends who experienced drastically different socioeconomic realities, though with common themes tying them together. And this enhanced nostalgic value makes more painful the thought of their being simply tossed into a dumpster and forgotten like so much other junk that can't be kept. Even just the musty smell of the old black-and-whites is part of their unique charm and value, which will be missed. And here again the fleeting nature of these things is keenly highlighted, and thereby the ironic fine line between trash and treasure.

Speaking of fine lines, another in relation to this subject is the one which serves as a kind of event horizon—which is to say the point of no return—separating how you relate to and think of your loved ones both before and after they die. That is, in a way true to the old saying *You don't know what you've got until it's gone*, confronting this reality firsthand, rather than merely hypothetically, causes you to reflect on the permanence and profundity of it in a way that you can't until you've actually lost the person. If love bites, death devours. No matter how mentally prepared for these monumental turning points you may or may not be when they happen, there is a surreal quality to the experience that stays with you from that point forward—or at least presumably it does, judging by how it feels several months thereafter, in conjunction with what others in the same boat have also mentioned feeling in this regard many years afterward. As my cousin Brian put it recently, the day after losing his own mother (less than three weeks after we lost ours, and a year after having lost his father): "There is a finality to know that I now exist completely without either of my parents on this earth." That is (at the risk of pointing out the obvious), there is all the difference in the world between the idea of and the actual reality of a person's permanent absence, especially when it comes to those we cherish most.

This is often most true regarding our parents, with whom in most cases we share the closest among all our relationships, since we are generally the recipients of their love and care the longest of any of these—not to mention the fact that it is through them (by the miraculous grace and power of God) that we receive the gift of life itself, and are therefore a composite of the two—which by itself puts them in a category of their own in this regard. And because we don't like to spend much time dwelling on the unwelcome fact of their inevitable permanent departure from this life, we grow comfortable with the privilege of taking for granted not knowing what life is like without them, until all of a sudden one day they are gone, and the more time passes the more it sinks in what an invaluable treasure they were—past tense—and how impoverished we feel in their absence. As often as you want to ask them simple things like what exactly they put in the lasagna or rice pudding to give it that particular flavor and consistency you can never quite replicate, or who all the strange faces (presumably relatives) are in that photo album from the 1800s, or you need trustworthy, battle-tested advice about how to be a better spouse or parent, or even when you just want to pick up the phone and hear their voice again, that's all, just one more time, or tell them what's new lately or chat about the superficial and mundane—you realize that that door is not only no longer wide open, it is firmly shut for good. It even takes some cajoling to force yourself to erase their name and number from your phone, which feels wrong, almost like a betrayal—to allow yourself to think the thought that you'll never call that number again. It may prove somewhat cathartic to mumble to yourself now and then as if in conversation with them what you never had the courage or took the opportunity to get off your chest, or just to joke with them about some quirk of theirs that you have inherited, but this only does you so much good. Sooner or later you have to come to grips with the realization that you won't be seeing them wave goodbye any longer from the living room window or driveway as you back away toward home after yet another pleasant visit, nor will you probably ever pull into or out of that driveway again—though presumably nostalgia will one day beckon you to slowly drive by and take a good long look, maybe even stopping briefly to talk with the new owners if they're outside. But for now, from here on out, all you can do is gratefully savor all the precious memories, occasionally giving way to the tears as you fumble through photo albums or make passing comments to friends or colleagues, "as Dad used to say" or "like Mom loved to do." And while this kind of head-on confrontation with the implications of death can be painful and take time, even a long time, to heal, it can also have a surprising redeeming value that shapes your perspective in unique and positive ways, a value that wasn't possible as long as the ones you lost were still around. Another important value that often follows this experience is the tendency to contemplate more seriously what comes after death—specifically, the continuation of our conscious existence and the meeting of our Maker, including the potential consequences thereof, which for many will include regaining what would otherwise have been irredeemably lost— which hopefully impacts for the better the remaining time we have left.

And while all this Death Talk has a way of wearing you out and wanting a break from the topic, it can also help motivate you to start thinking about putting plans in place for yourself. I'm probably more prone than most my age to have done this kind of thinking and planning so early simply on account of my status as a quadriplegic, which for various reasons, from the very day I joined this demographic, has made me more susceptible than typical for someone my age to health-related threats, which over the course of the last three decades have nearly snuffed me out more times than I can count. So, prompted by the realization that I've put off this planning far too long, particularly in light of the additional, universally relevant fact that tomorrow is by no means guaranteed, I eventually took the bold first step of writing myself a note on my kitchen table, and in hindsight that by itself was crucial. Besides, the more you ponder the prospect of your loved ones losing you and all that that entails, and then, on top of the grief, having to start from scratch with the anxious, last-minute planning of what kind of service you would have wanted, as well as what to do with your stuff, you want to do what you can to help make that process as seamless as possible for them. And if you think there is anything else on your to-do list that you are more likely to put off than this—with the possible exceptions of a colonoscopy or having all your wisdom teeth pulled—you would be wrong, since of course meaning to do something and actually doing it are as different as life and death, even once you've got it written down. It turns out we don't much like to face the prospect of our own inevitable departure from this life—go figure—though actually it's probably the planning as much as anything that we fear.

And while I did well to write myself that first reminder, unfortunately, though predictably, it sat there for more months than I can recall before I finally picked up the phone to make an appointment. In my defense, though, aside from pure procrastination, the other reason, i.e. excuse, why it took so long to do this is that this note was simply one among several others, since I can apparently get nothing done anymore without first writing it down (this was before the unspeakably helpful convenience of smartphone reminders, whose persistence, if you hold out long enough, have a way of compelling you into action). And so, like new decorations on your walls or shelves, which stand out for a while at first, before long these notes blend in with everything else on the table (and mine is crowded with plenty of other stuff). However, occasionally friends—a fairly nosy bunch, I might add—

would notice them and ask, *Funeral plans?* and I would be re-minded and have to explain.

That was also about fifteen years ago now, and the one thing in particular I remember from that first appointment, sitting across from the nameless, faceless sport jacket tucked cozily within the horseshoe of his desk, are the handful of cartoonish, pinky-tall figurines lurking on the shelf behind him, what looked like the clever personalities from some animated children's movie or TV show I had never heard of, the kind of promotional collect-ibles fast-food joints used to give away when I was a kid, except in this case, oddly and ironically enough, the theme of this little fam-ily appeared to be Death. They weren't zombies, though, just ghoulish, with expressions less dreadful than friendly, like *The Munsters* or *The Addams Family,* right out in the open to be seen by every potential customer or client, or whatever you call the person on my side of the desk. And while admittedly my expecta-tions of such a setting were pretty neutral, this little display didn't exactly exude an aura of credibility or reverence, which is proba-bly the least that the average person expects. At any rate, I don't remember the tone of the meeting fitting that kooky theme, or an-ything creepy or otherwise abnormal about the man himself—though with all respect to the profession, there is, in any case, something a little eerie about it, however practical and essential it may be, especially as you try to imagine those who devote their lives to it undertaking its necessary duties. Anyhow, the warp and woof of all this is that, though I had finally taken the initiative to get there, I only came away with more questions to think over, with the hope of getting back there fairly soon to complete the deal, the idea being to make the most of the momentum already set in motion.

And guess how that went?

On the positive side, I came home with a lap full of paperwork and pamphlets to peruse, along with the notes I took, all of which I conscientiously and deliberately placed on my kitchen table directly across from where I eat, a spot I pass by many times a day. Surely this would sooner than later induce me to make a follow-up appointment to tie up the remaining loose ends (actually, loose ends were all there were at that point). But like the reminder notes sitting right in front of me every time I ate, before long this shallow stack of information got covered up by one thing and then another, so it wound up taking me a good decade (no joke) to muster the ambition to rummage through that pile again and make another appointment (are you surprised, by the way, that a stack of papers could rest in relative peace and harmony that long in one spot on a bachelor's kitchen table? In my defense, I cite the only line I remember from *Moby Dick*: "There are some enterprises in which a careful disorderliness is the true method"). And when at last I made the call, I was informed that the funeral home had changed owners, so I pretty much had to start again from scratch, which doesn't exactly do wonders for your motivation.

Fortunately, however, it was around this time that a buddy of mine and I had the providential opportunity to attend an event on the topic one evening at our local YMCA. And while in light of my previous procrastination it seems implausible to me that we actually made plans beforehand to go, I accept my friend's recollection over my own because, while both of our memories of the occasion are fuzzy, mine seems the more unlikely (that we were just passing by and spontaneously decided to drop in). At any rate, we entered the large room from the rear, doing our best to creep in quietly behind what appeared to be a rapt audience of mostly gray or balding heads, the session apparently already in progress. Receiving from the greeters a brochure and agenda, we hung near the back as each of the sharp-suited salesmen took turns pacing back and forth with microphone in hand, preaching the gospel of preemptive funeral and legal estate planning. Several scenarios and program options were laid out by each in accord with their own particular field of expertise, with a mutual emphasis upon the critically important need for proactive planning. That is, unless a guy or gal is indifferent to the prospect of being taken to the cleaners by Uncle Sam or some unscrupulous relative or lawyer, simply on account of dying in America in the twenty-first century—rather, dying without having done sufficient planning; or, worse yet, no planning at all.

Soon overwhelmed by the multitude of details, and probably also the unsettling fact of my own ill-preparedness, it wasn't long before my attention wandered across the ostensibly captivated crowd, noting how few people my age there were (most were at least my friend's age, twenty-three years my senior). The other, maybe more unfortunate thing that struck me was the fact that this is how I, someone who considers himself not altogether without a social life, chose to spend a summer evening. I also remember thinking how funny it would be to meet your spouse at such an event, what a romantic story you'd have to share thereafter— *Yeah, we met at a symposium for planning each other's deaths.* But the main takeaway for me seemed to be how complicated and costly it's become just to die in America in this day and age. Here in the so-called modern, civilized West, even the rural Midwest.

Though I suppose comparing all the options and laws regulating this realm to the tax code would probably be an overstatement, still the process isn't nearly as simple and straightforward as one could hope. And sitting there I couldn't help but think of so many multitudes in diverse countries and cultures worldwide who surely live so much more simply when it comes to these things, where in all likelihood there is no need whatsoever to spend much time, money, or energy concerned about such details, where a guy can just close his eyes and be laid in the ground by his family and local community without having to bother so much with all the rigmarole of buying a casket and tombstone and plot of land, to say nothing of the scores of other details involved in services which might be held, or the distribution of whatever the person has left behind, including any potential legal matters to settle (other than property or livestock, they probably don't have stocks, bonds, 401(k), IRA, or life insurance to worry about). Likewise, go back a hundred or five hundred years or more, anywhere you please—just imagine how much simpler things must have been in this regard. In light of which we should recognize how rare and unique a society we just happened to be allowed the opportunity to experience, both for better and for worse.

Speaking of simplicity in this regard, I am sometimes reminded of a few notable biblical characters and how uncomplicated it appears to have been for people to die in their day. Consider the old patriarch Jacob near the end (circa 1876 B.C.), who, after blessing each of his twelve sons, said, "I am to be gathered to my people; bury me with my fathers in the cave that is in the field of Ephron the Hittite,"[1] where his father, Isaac, and grandfather, Abraham, who bought the cave, and their spouses were buried. More remarkably, immediately after this it says, "he drew his feet into the bed and breathed his last and was gathered to his people"[2]—which seems to indicate he had some intimation that it was his time to go right there and then. In a similar way, Moses is commanded directly by God, "Go up this mountain of the Abarim ... and die on the mountain which you go up, and be gathered to your people"[3]—and that's just what he did, as casually as if he were climbing into bed for the night. This also happened somewhat similarly for his brother, Aaron,[4] and in one sense there is something almost comical about it, the idea of someone—the Author of life itself, no less—saying, "go up there and die," and then the person does. No worries about planning a memorial ceremony or getting a will legally notarized or anything of the like. Jacob did give directions concerning his bones, that they be carried back to Canaan (i.e. Israel) to be buried in the tomb just mentioned, but that's about as complicated as it got for his funeral planning, if you can call it that. Neither did the Lord Jesus Christ worry one whit about any of it, trusting his Father for his every need, and when the appointed hour arrived, along came Nicodemus and Joseph of Arimathea as if by special arrangement, risking their necks to receive his corpse from Governor Pilate, binding him in linen cloths with burial spices according to the Jewish custom, and laying him in Joseph's own tomb.[5]

And while these examples are simply to emphasize simpler times and ways, no matter where you live, or when, how much hassle you have to deal with in this regard really depends on how much you own, and to what degree you care about what happens to it all in your absence. This being the case, you have to wonder why more people don't live more simply, or just decide to give it away or spend it all before they get too old. In one sense it's a good thing that we have some of the laws and red tape that we do, so that the inevitable disputes can be settled in a civil, legal way, as opposed to a kind of law-of-the-jungle, might-makes-right policy, which undoubtedly has been the historical norm in most cultures worldwide since ancient times. This makes you wonder how much these things have changed over the last century or so, especially here, and how and when things began to become more complicated.

And while the more you have certainly tends to complicate end-of-life planning, as it has come to be called, still, for the average American Joe, despite how little he leaves behind, dying isn't cheap. According to the National Funeral Directors Association (NFDA) Member General Price List Study, in 2021 the national median cost for a funeral with a viewing and burial service was roughly $7848, while the same thing involving cremation was about $6970. That cost includes things as essential as the removal/transfer of "the remains" to the funeral home or cemetery or church, use of facilities and staff for viewing and a ceremony, and options like memorial cards or a register book.[6] Of course, this cost will depend on whether or not you want a casket or urn, and what each of these are made out of. And this doesn't even include the burial plot, headstone, and (if necessary) concrete vault, or the cost to feed any attendees after the service. As with buying a car, there are plentiful options to consider in every respect, and the cost adds up just as quickly. On the other hand, however, though in some sense the costs for these services can seem expensive to us, imagine the alternative of having to having to undertake the burial of our loved ones by ourselves, as multitudes have done for ages and continue to do all over the world. Cleaning up the body, handling it, transporting it, laying it in the ground. So probably this service that we take for granted is a much greater and more cost-effective blessing than we realize.

While we're on the subject, a few other interesting tidbits might as well be mentioned, for whatever they're worth. According to the 2021 NFDA Cremation & Burial Report—which, if you're interested, can be purchased by nonmembers of the NFDA in digital format for a mere $175—the cremation rate for 2021 was projected to be 57.5%, compared with 36.6% for traditional burial.[7] And in 2015, for the first time in U. S. history, the national casketed burial rate (45.2%) was surpassed by the cremation rate (47.9%).[8] Not only that, the 2020 NFDA Report predicted that by 2040 the cremation rate in the U. S. will skyrocket to 78%, leaving the number of casketed burials to account for only 16% of deaths.[9] To put this in perspective, consider that the cremation rates in 1960, 1990, and 2010 were 3.6%, 17.1%, and 40.4%, respectively.[10] The NFDA website also mentions the fairly recent phenomenon of so-called "green funerals,"[11] for the eco-conscious—fear not, tree-huggers (and probably vegans) of the world, you can now rest in peace with a clean, green conscience. This might or might not involve carpooling, gathering in a natural setting, locally-grown organic flowers and food, formaldehyde-free embalming or recycled paper products, or a biodegradable casket. Even traditional headstones are forsaken in favor of plants, trees, or rocks. In America, of all places—who could have guessed?

But back to my own planning. Eventually I got around to making that appointment with the new funeral guy down the street, and this time we got some things nailed down in pretty short order. Slowly perusing through the brochures with me as he answered my questions, the director took notes and ticked off the pertinent boxes in accord with my preferences, even as I wondered with each stroke of the pen what the total would be. And no matter which options you choose, in a strange way the whole process feels like ordering from a most unappetizing menu (*I think I'll have the immediate burial, please, with a side of indifference*). The only real preference I had was to keep things as simple and natural as possible, though not quite the "green" route, the existence of which at the time I was unaware, nor did I notice it as an option on the template form. Although neither cremation nor being filled with man-made preservatives before burial seemed appealing, thinking these to be my only options, I came in prepared to settle for one or the other. But then I had the audacity to ask if there was any other option, and I cited the example of how Jews in first-century Palestine did things, as far as I was aware: first, laying the body in a tomb, then, about a year later, collecting the bones and putting them into a wooden or stone box called an ossuary. I wasn't suggesting I wanted this option (though I might if I had a tomb handy), but mentioning it prompted the director to suggest something similar, namely what the local Muslims apparently do, simply wrapping the body in a sheet and laying it in the grave, flush against the earth, covered only by the required concrete vault and more earth. Perfect, I thought (though upon further honest reflection, it's hard not to admit that this option seems to fit the "green" category, in spite of my tongue-in-cheek desire not to be in any way affiliated with either tree-huggers or vegans). So, after paying for the vault and the specific piece of real estate where my bones will lie until Jesus returns—which I chose from a plethora of numbered slots indicated on a large blueprint sheet shown me by the owner of the cemetery (for kicks I picked a spot in the sunshine)—my mission had finally been accomplished. Or almost. Sooner than later I also got together with that legal estate planner I had seen at the Y several years before and got my Living Will officially written up and notarized.

Now all that remains is the inevitable, the day of reckoning when all this effort pays off, and it's a relief to know that, aside from a few minor details like which songs I'd like sung at the memorial service or which scripture to put on my tombstone (my preferences keep changing every several months), there's no more planning to bother about. Now the only thing that occasionally crosses my mind along these lines is how exactly I and those closest to me that remain will make our ultimate departure (incidentally, in less time than it's taken to write this essay, eight close family members, including both of my parents, have recently made said departure). As natural as it is to wonder about this, it's not something a person dwells upon very long, because of course the road ahead is unwritten and beyond our control, which means, with few exceptions (like some of the biblical patriarchs), we don't know when our number is up, or if we will leave the scene peacefully or otherwise. It's certainly a fascinating phenomenon when we hear of contemporary examples of people seeming to know the end is near and then passing as if on cue, as actually happened with my Uncle Bob fairly recently, who, after his health took a sudden turn for the worst and his wife and kids were alerted so they could tell him one last time that they loved him and that it was okay to go Home and rest in peace with Jesus, he slipped away an hour later. Mysterious for sure, and probably not common, but for real nonetheless. At any rate, most of us hope that we and those we love will live a long, happy life into old age without enduring too much pain or discomfort and then pass away peacefully like that. But that's not always the way of things, is it? It's pretty incredible to think that there are multitudes who pass from this life without ever having grieved the loss of a loved one, while scores of others have outlived nearly everyone they've loved, and unfortunately had to suffer through more loss than seems fair for anyone. Another thing that comes to mind now and then that is just as natural to wonder about is who will go first, and last, in the family (nuclear and extended), and what the implications will be afterward in each scenario. Depending on who goes when, the dynamics of the family change necessarily and uniquely. It's not so much the first one to go that I'm prone to think of as much as the last one. What will it be like for that solitary one who has outlived the others? Will it be one of the parents or the children? Will they wish they had gone first, or at least before last? Again, this is not something we usually dwell on for very long. Time will tell. And in the meantime, one way or the other, whatever God's plan may be, there's no good reason to waste time and energy fretting about it.

---

[1] Gen. 49:29

[2] Gen. 49:33

[3] Deut. 32:48-50

[4] Num. 2:20-29

[5] John 19:38-42

[6] National Funeral Directors Association, "2021 NFDA General Price List Study Shows Funeral Costs Not Rising as Fast as Rate of Inflation," Nov. 4, 2021, https://nfda.org/news/media-center/nfda-news-releases/id/6182 /2021-nfda-general-price-list-study-shows-funeral-costs-not-rising-as-fast-as-rate-of-inflation.

[7] National Funeral Directors Association, 2021, https://nfda.org/news/statistics.

[8] National Funeral Directors Association, "2020 Cremation & Burial Projects Cremation Rate of 87% by 2040," Jul. 6, 2020, https://nfda.org/news /in-the-news/nfda-news/id/5223/2020-cremation-burial-projects-cremation-rate-of-87-by-2040.

[9] Ibid.

[10] Davis Funeral Home, Accessed Mar. 5, 2023, https://www.davisfuneralhomenh.com/benefits-of-cremation.

[11] National Funeral Directors Association, Accessed Nov. 30, 2022, https://nfda.org/resources/business-technical/green-funeral-practices/what-it-means-to-be-green.

Time for Livin'

In view of these circumstances, it is no matter for surprise that, when we ask people even to consider the possibility of decadence, we meet incredulity and resentment. We must consider that we are in effect asking for a confession of guilt and an acceptance of sterner obligation; we are making demands in the name of the ideal or the suprapersonal, and we cannot expect a more cordial welcome than disturbers of complacency have received in any other age. On the contrary, our welcome will rather be less today, for a century and a half of bourgeois ascendancy has produced a type of mind highly unreceptive to unsettling thoughts. Added to this is the egotism of modern man, fed by many springs, which will scarcely permit the humility needed for self-criticism.

—Richard M. Weaver, *Ideas Have Consequences*

She sauntered right up to me out of nowhere—more than a decade ago, a total stranger in her twenties, a caregiver for one of my neighbors, into the multi-windowed community room where I spend so many sunny winter afternoons—just to ask, with all-too-typical flippancy: *Excuse me, do you have Wi-Fi?*

Like in my apartment, she meant. To which she could connect, if I wouldn't mind—and why would I? Except that I didn't know her from Eve, and that her unsmiling monotone, her inability to look away from the phone for which she was petitioning, her lack of any further conversation whatsoever, all seemed plainly to indicate that my sole value consisted in my potential possession of this precious, apparently scarce resource.

This caught me off guard. Borrowing Wi-Fi, of all things (if *borrowing* is the right word)? And from a stranger? I guess I was more out of touch with the current culture and generations beneath me than I realized.

And yet, stranger still, I heard myself without the slightest hesitation answer, *Yeah*, and then just as quickly and inexplicably followed up her *Do you mind if I use it?* with *No, go ahead*, and gave her my SSID and password. A complete stranger—did I mention that? As if it were required by law, or the polite thing to do under the circumstances, or part of a tit-for-tat arrangement, or from fear that my refusal might cause her to frown and turn around and walk away without another word. God in heaven forbid!

At any rate it was a first that left me baffled, wondering what to make of it, wondering what to make of myself—such a pushover, such an easy sell—asking myself things like: *Have we really come to this? Have I really come to this?*

And instantly my mind flashed back to a similar memorable occasion not long before this, which happened during an otherwise routine and uneventful stroll downtown as I casually approached an intersection, where some young man, like so many others, walking blindly toward me in broad daylight with his phone in front of his face, made me wonder, if I didn't say something, would he run smack into me? But just in the nick of time I said, *Hey there*, and his eyes managed to glance up just long enough to allow him to sidestep me as you would a steaming pile.

This naturally made me ponder the whole way home what kind of world this is turning into, what kind of a society, where, to give another example, or symptom, thereof, it's no longer unusual to see boys and girls under ten years old on skateboards and scooters, bicycles and even little tricycles, for heaven's sake, riding one-handed as they're talking and texting and, from what I'm told, "sexting," and who knows what else they're doing on these devices, which part of me really doesn't want to know. Though that's not so good either, just ignoring things without saying a word—*Que Sera, Sera*—whistling past the cemetery, as they say.

And while venting about this feels entirely justified and slightly satisfying—whether just on paper or in conversation with friends and family my age or older, who by and large feel similarly, acknowledging what seem like mostly negative trends—it does next to nothing to actually address the issue. But beyond noticing and venting, mostly privately, what more can the average person really do? Especially when you consider that most every one of us is to one degree or other complicit in this new fad, if that's all this is. Or should we just leave the real work to the psycho-social experts and Ivy League institutions with their endless PhDs, dissertations, and case studies to tell us which trends and tendencies do and do not qualify as substantial threats to our so-called civilized way of life? Back when these things were first becoming undeniably obvious to anyone paying the slightest attention, and the conviction grew strong enough in me to inspire the makings of an editorial, a chance to shine what seemed to me to be some much-needed light on the issue, hoping without much expectation for the best, and I asked a trusted friend for feedback to make sure I wasn't off my rocker in a fit of unwarranted cynicism, the response was: *There are bigger fish to fry*. Which, of course, is nearly always true, and therefore impossible to argue with, even when you have the energy and inclination to do so, which at the time I did not. And just like that the article died on the operating table. So much for trying to do my small part.

But back to the girl walking away from me under the spell-binding influence of my Wi-Fi like a junkie from her sugar daddy, a barely audible *thank you* possibly lingering in her wake. Something else struck me as she quickly disappeared, the result of some of the homework I had done for that waste of a potential editorial that went nowhere and accomplished little more than to make me aware of a behavioral trend I had neither heard of nor thought possible, called *Nomophobia*. Go ahead, google it. An odd term, to be sure, coined during the course of certain scientific studies done at the time in England and Europe, to describe a particular tendency among many who allegedly fear the state of being left with *no mo*bile connection, which is to say no internet—no access to relieve their constant creature cravings that compel them even to approach, if necessary, absolute strangers to get their fix. After all, who can fathom living without such for even thirty consecutive seconds in this constantly evolving, and de-volving, techno-toxicated age?

And if this particular tendency was true then, how many more such studies have been done in the meantime, revealing in more pages and nitty-gritty details and newly coined terms than most of us would care to read all the unsettling propensities human beings have sunk to in this regard since then? About which so few seem to be either aware or concerned, at least enough to move beyond simple observation, diagnosis, and education to actually addressing the issues as a culture, from the least to the greatest among us. Even if that means pointing the accusatory finger back at ourselves, so that it doesn't feel so often like you are witnessing the real-time destruction of this present age and culture right before your very eyes. Or am I still just as apparently out of touch as I was a decade ago? Granted, there are certainly still bigger fish out there to fry, and I'm by no means a behavioral scientist—though evidently I have some armchair aspirations—but in the meantime, where's the harm in frying up a small fish, if that's all this is, though I have my doubts? If, at the very least, what follows has anything to say about where we're at and where we're headed as a culture and country, we ought not feel ashamed for probing a little deeper and asking a few more questions.

I'm not sure what troubles me most about the tendencies I'm witnessing more and more regularly these days, nor am I sure *which* of these tendencies trouble me most. The main thing, I think, is continuing to see more and more people—not just teenagers and twenty-somethings anymore—so absorbed by these "smart" phones, so completely distracted from what's going on immediately around them, and apparently perfectly content this way. Positively blissful, it would seem, zoned out, staring like idiots, periodically smiling, smirking, from time to time laughing out loud, often without realizing or seeming to care if anyone near them hears, even when there's no one on the other end. Just them and their inanimate device, isolated in their own private little world, no matter how many people surround them, anytime they are on their way anywhere, as they leave a building until they reach their car, or vice versa, or while standing in line somewhere, even while driving, despite knowing the dangers of doing so, both for themselves and for others, not to mention the laws against this. And the more I see it, the more it irks me, to the point that I sometimes imagine walking right up and tearing the thing away from them, smashing it to pieces at their feet or throwing it as far as possible, indoors or outdoors, with or without an audience. I freely admit this is surely not what Jesus had in mind when he told us to love our neighbor as ourselves, though on the other hand, what about the old adage that says honesty is the best policy? Not that I would ever do it, even if I were physically able. But the mere thought of the horrified look on the person's face is alone sufficient to spark such a fantasy, in which I indulge more often than I care to admit.

Or what about the seeming corollary to this self-inflicted state of isolation, namely the lag time between the moment you try to get the attention of one so engrossed and the moment they actually respond. Most of the time it takes five or more seconds before they even lift their face, looking somewhat dazed, even drugged, as though returning to the surface from a deep dive, and ask you to repeat whatever you just said. Of course, someone might reasonably object: *What's the big deal about a few seconds? So what if I don't respond immediately?* Fair enough. But those of us old enough to remember shouldn't forget that, even just a decade or so ago, when people were not so continually preoccupied, their response times were generally much more immediate, and the source of their distraction was not repeatedly the exact same thing. Moreover, the very fact that such unwitting slaves so quickly, as if by involuntary reflex, return their attention back to their device after such interruptions is an obvious indication that this observation has merit.

Another troubling trend you see occasionally is the sudden look of panic that overtakes the expression of one so blissfully immersed when they realize, too late, that their battery is on the verge of dying, or dead—or, worse yet, they forgot their charger. Frantically searching their pockets, their purse, their backpack and every square inch around them, eventually their dismayed gaze falls on you as they unwittingly state the fact aloud, as if their child is lost and you might be able to help. By lending them *your* charger, that is, for which they waste no time asking—stranger though you may be—though you have to inform them, without a single ounce of regret, that you don't carry one with you every-where you go (perish the thought!). Part of you hates to admit how amusing and gratifying it is to watch them worry and fuss over something that is in the grand scheme of things so patheti-cally unimportant and unnecessary. For a moment it almost feels like cosmic justice on a small scale, a humiliating blow against all the disquieting trends in their collective entirety. But this satis-faction is short-lived, since another moment's reflection is all it takes to make you realize, deep down, that what you're witness-ing really isn't funny, it's tragic. Just another symptom of the larger epidemic. Just another human being made in God's image reduced by their own lack of discretion to voluntary servitude, to dependence on an inanimate object—an idol in many cases, to be sure—to such a degree that it seems to take precedence over all their other concerns, sometimes including their children. Which makes you wonder what they might be willing to give or do at mo-ments like these in exchange for what they're convinced they so desperately need.

But for the record, don't waste your breath trying to suggest to such a one—family, friend, acquaintance, or stranger—that the device on which they seem so constantly prone to rely might have any degree of control over them, or that their persistent preoccu-pation therewith in any way precludes their ability either to focus or to multitask. You'll sooner convince them to stop using the thing altogether. After all, such ideas conjure up hideous labels with which no one cares to be associated: *compulsion, obsession, addiction.*

And don't forget the increasingly ubiquitous trend of head-phones—more recently, earbuds—so many are wearing like the latest fashion statement practically twenty-four-seven these days (I have no doubt that many sleep with them in). If cell phones—especially smartphones—alone so often prove to be a deterrent to normal interactions between human beings within close proximity, this new trend only makes it that much more difficult, because now a person's ears, in addition to their eyes, are likewise distracted and closed off to the outside world. In fact, as far as nonverbal communication is concerned, the very presence of these in a person's ears—the same way as the phone in their hand—essentially says, *Do Not Disturb.* Of course, headphones have been a popular trend for decades, but now it's not just young people and those who exercise who use them, but people of almost every demographic, and in nearly every social situation, personal or professional. However, they do have the redeeming value of preventing some, who apparently feel they are at home everywhere they go, from playing their music or videos or speakerphone conversations aloud, which I witness on an all-too-regular basis. And yet surprisingly you'll sometimes still be able to engage such a person, though only after they take a moment to stop whatever they are watching or listening to, sometimes even offering you the added courtesy of removing their earpiece(s) entirely. But more often (at least in my experience)—and this is another one that really gets me—as you're talking with them, they suddenly pause, break eye-contact, and say something that doesn't seem to fit your conversation, followed by something else, until you're forced to say, *Are you talking to me?* and with a smile they point to their ear and lip-synch something that makes you nod with the realization that they apparently have more important business to attend to than the likes of you. Then, ten seconds or two minutes later, out of nowhere, reestablishing eye-contact, they start talking to you again as though there hadn't been any interruption, so that once again you have to ask, *Are you talking to me?* And this is just one more symptom of the larger epidemic, and yet another, it would seem, on the increase.

Then there's an associated phenomenon frequently faced by most of the young men I observe up close on a regular basis (my caregivers). Usually sooner than later after having worked their shift, they will text or call or knock on the door, looking for their earbuds or charger or phone, and you have to stop whatever you're doing to take a quick look through every room, or stand by watching them do the same, rummaging over every surface, shuffling papers and sometimes overturning the cushions of your sofa, only to discover, nearly every time, *Nope, not here.* Of course, in one sense this is no big deal. It happens to everyone at some point with their wallet or purse or keys. But in this case it only started happening a few years ago, and now continues to happen on a fairly regular basis—in this specific case to young men in their teens through thirties, though I have no doubt that this trend, like the rest, cuts across nearly every demographic. And so lately, as they are leaving, I've actually been compelled into the habit of asking, as if their mother, *Got everything?*

Another thing I've been surprised to notice more frequently among the under-forty crowd is the fairly recent, but so far rare, phenomenon of carrying *two* phones—always smartphones, of course. I'm not referring to people like my nurse, who in addition to her own phone is required to carry one in connection with her job (apparently reluctantly, judging from her sighs and grumbles every time it vibrates, dings, or rings—also through her touchscreen watch). I'm talking about individuals who, for whatever reason—and to spare myself the inane justifications, I've stopped asking why—*choose* to have two. Actually, I did recently notice one reason some do this—can you guess? So they can talk on one while staring at the other, of course. I kid you not, I actually witnessed this, surprisingly for the first time. Which, of course, means that when one isn't dinging or ringing, the other one is. And it's not like there isn't enough dinging and ringing with just one! Man, don't I sound like a crabby old coot?

If some of this sounds like exaggeration for the sake of firming up the argument, I invite you to pull up a chair at my kitchen table this evening as I eat dinner. The only thing distinguishing this particular experience from any other day of the week is that I have two caregivers working this shift instead of one, the second being a new trainee. Both young men are under thirty, and both are sloppily stretched out on my couch, fully absorbed in their screens, not saying a word to one another or to me. The "trainer" has the volume blaring, what sounds like the quirky noises of a videogame combined with several voices he is simultaneously talking to on speakerphone, presumably his opponents, who are each in separate countries: Somalia, Saudi Arabia, and Greece. He seems altogether indifferent as to whether this racket is appropriate either on the job or in the company of others, let alone in someone else's home, or in this case all three—in particular the home of the very one whose approval or disapproval will ultimately determine whether or not he remains employed. The device of the trainee is silent, though it's unclear whether he is choosing to be courteous or simply guarding his privacy, or if he just has an earbud in that I can't see. Ironically, it's times like this when you're actually *thankful* for the earbuds, and later suggest to the one without them to maybe think about getting some—to which he responds that he can't, because they would hurt his ears, which makes you wonder if he means the sound or simply having the things crammed in there, though such a response drains any inclination to clarify further. A moment later I ask for some help, and after a few seconds they each, like a pair of sunflowers, reluctantly lift and turn their languid faces—first at me, then at one another—staring for a long moment as if mutually hoping the other will volunteer himself. Finally, prompted by the nod of his trusty trainer, the trainee slowly rises. It only takes two seconds for him to help me, and the moment he finishes, before he even turns to take his first step back to the couch, guess what? Out comes the phone. Then *my* phone rings, which I take on speakerphone as I always must, and even after my first minute or two talking, the blaring background noise is neither reduced nor stopped. And if I weren't curious as to whether or not that might change over the next several minutes, I would politely ask him to please turn it down or off. But in the interest of science I let it ride, and after ten minutes of trying to talk over the undiminished cacophony, I can't help wondering if, God forbid, I should start choking on my chicken nuggets, how long it would take either of these technophiles (nomophobes?) to notice. Suddenly I find myself chewing much more carefully.

At any rate, the more you witness scenes like this, the more you hope, however ineffectually, that such folks take several multi-minute breaks from their screens at least a few times a day. You would like to hope that a coherent presentation of anecdotes and statistics in this regard might help convince them of the immensity and pervasiveness of this multifaceted epidemic, though this is probably pushing the limits of glass-half-full thinking. Which brings to mind another timeless gem by Richard Weaver: "Surely we are justified in saying of our time: If you seek the monument to our folly, look about you."[1] More than that, it's all a reminder of just how much the world has changed, and rapidly continues to change, compared to the one in which you grew up, or even the one just a little more than a decade ago. It makes you wonder if this is how your parents' and grandparents' generations felt as they witnessed the almost equally sudden, overwhelming arrival of the landline telephone, radio, and television. It also makes you wonder if this current explosion of newfangled products and tendencies—created and utilized by the constituents of a drastically different era and culture than the former—should be analyzed and judged according to similar or different standards.

Whatever you may think about it, this is where we are at the present moment, where we have arrived through an innumerable series of incremental steps from a time and place not so long ago that I remember fondly, when people walking down the street or riding the bus together or seeing one another at the store were more likely—because they were less preoccupied—to engage one another, and with more than just half-polite funeral smiles and nods, even if only about mundane things like the weather or how one another is doing. After all, it's not like we're an urban hotbed along either of the coasts, where trends like this are expected to show up, like acne on a teenager. All this is happening here, as much as anywhere, in the rural Midwest, and that fact alone should make us sit up and pay closer attention.

It's hard to keep up these days with the pace at which the changes are happening technologically. No matter how new your smartphone or tablet is, the next upgrade will be ready within a year, if that. I feel out of my element in this brave new world, so I can't imagine what it must be like for those older than I am. I often thank God for the privilege of having to scrape tooth and nail through the undignified Stone Age of my K-12 education without so much as a home computer (I know, can you believe it?). Aside from the radio and television, the closest thing to an information superhighway we had in our household was a dusty old rack of encyclopedias Mom bought from a door-to-door salesman just after we kids were born. And while my Gen X classmates and I grew up taking for granted life without either internet or our own cell phones, we weren't the only ones so deprived. In that respect we were in the same primitive boat as the petrified generations above us. Even doctors and lawyers in those days relied mostly on pagers, which still required use of a landline telephone, even up through the nineties. When cell phones did become available, few had them, maybe partly because they were (no joke) practically the size of your head and looked like military walkie-talkies.[2, 3] Given the current ubiquity of cell phones we now take for granted, it's astounding to realize, and important to remember, again with the help of Google, that the prevalence of cell phone use as we now know it didn't really begin—and even then fairly gradually—until the early 2000s, by which time most of my high school classmates and I had already graduated college—and the arrival of the touchscreen not until the end of that decade. Which is, of course, the point from which everything has since exploded—the number of devices and apps available, the number of users, and most notably the manifold increase in the frequency with which people are using them.

Aside from some early touchscreens making their cameos in the nineties, including the first, IBM's Simon Personal Communicator (1992), and the Palm Pilot (1997), the so-called capacitive touchscreen smartphone didn't emerge until 2007, with the original iPhone.[4, 5] In fact, it's startling to think that all the big corporate names we take mostly for granted nowadays, which play such pivotal roles in countless lives in the worldwide political, economic, and pop-cultural system, are hardly two decades old: LinkedIn (2002), Facebook (2004), YouTube (2005), Twitter (2006), WhatsApp (2009), Instagram (2010), Snapchat (2011), TikTok (2016). If you can believe it, even Google, which didn't take long to become a verb so many of us use almost daily, just showed up on the scene in 1998, shortly after Yahoo and Amazon, both in 1994. There are many others, of course, and new ones emerging fairly consistently, but contrary to how well-established and indispensable any or all of these entities seem and how many users they have, we have only just embarked on this global experiment, the ultimate consequences of which are only beginning to be measured and digested.

What's more, even for a generation as recent as my own, for so long it was normal to live without the nonstop preoccupation that cell phones—especially smartphones—have made possible, not to mention predictable. Back then, as often as situations inevitably arose when you couldn't think of certain facts of math or science, history, geography, politics or popular culture, it was normal not to have immediate access at your fingertips to answer every conceivable question. Mostly you had to be content to live without such knowledge for the time being, until the next time you came into contact with the right person or book or radio or television tidbit that could enlighten your ignorance. If you were not at home and wanted to connect with family or friends, you had to find the nearest landline, usually at home. I suppose we scarcely could have believed it if you had suggested to us then that there would soon be an invisible sort of platform floating somewhere you don't know, containing more information than all the world's libraries combined (and then some), on which we would be posting "selfies" and every other experience under the sun, and by means of which we would instantly satisfy every curiosity and resolve nearly every dispute, all the while paying far too little attention to the veracity of the sources of such information. Sophisticated as we thought we were back then, we were practically Neanderthals compared to everything we take for granted these days, when Google, Siri, and Alexa have not only become part of our vocabulary, they've almost literally become part of the family—in fact I'll dare to venture that there are a great many out there who interact with these mysterious entities more than they do with actual human beings, even those closest to them (most without wondering whether these entities might in fact be conducting twenty-four-seven surveillance on them, though plenty of others do so in spite of the fact). And this is not even bringing into the conversation things like GPS or other forms of tracking, barcode and fingerprint and eye scanners, and who knows what else is going on in the palms of our hands that we don't even realize.[6,] [7] Speaking of which, who knows what all these meticulous user agreements bind us to, the ones we so often and so flippantly agree to with a thoughtless click without reading, which are surely deliberately made both sufficiently lengthy and technical to discourage our careful scrutiny, not to mention to cover the behinds of their authors. At the very least, we would do well to keep in the habit of reminding ourselves that the devil is very often in the details.

Even in the presumably pleasant company of family and friends nowadays—in gatherings small and large, private and public—it's already become normal to watch each other repeatedly pull out our phones to check our email or social media or the weather forecast or latest sports scores, or just to share pictures or videos of things we find funny or inspiring or contrary to democracy, or more often to show off the latest exploits of the kids or grandkids. The same way someone used to slip outside now and again for a cigarette they now disappear around a corner either to make or take some apparently critical call. Two or more people in the same room, even on the same couch or at the same table, will at one point or other be simultaneously engrossed with their devices, oblivious to one another. What's worse, by now we've all either witnessed or heard stories of people even this close "messaging" each other through their devices rather than interacting directly. We laugh at this on a superficial level, at the novelty and ridiculousness of it, a kind of fun-loving form of collective self-deprecation. But the undeniable reality is that people's increasing reliance on, obsession with, and addiction to these devices has already begun to affect how we engage with and relate to one another. And mind you, that's not just the opinion of a mere fryer of small fish. These things have been and continue to be all-too-well documented by far more credible sources than yours truly, and not just within the U. S.

But since our focus here does happen to be within the States, let's have a quick look at a modest sample of data, shall we? For starters, a 2021 Pew survey revealed that 97% of Americans own a cell phone of some kind,[8] which is probably the least controversial statistic among the rest since cell phones have for the most part replaced landline phones. That same year the number of smartphone owners was 85%[9]—specifically, 96% of those 18-29 years old, 95% of those 30-49, 83% of those 50-64, and 61% of those 65 and older[10]—which has increased substantially (93%) since 2012, as have each of the individual categories since then (18-29: up 46%; 30-49: up 61%; 50-64: up 144%; 65+: up 369%).[11] It's also worth mentioning that the percentage gap between the youngest and oldest categories has shrunk from 53 points in 2012 to 35 now.[12] This is significant because typically we think of the latest technology trends affecting mostly younger populations. As for American teens, since 2018 about 95% have, or have access to, a smartphone (compared with 73% in 2014-2015),[13] and currently 46% use the internet "almost constantly," which has nearly doubled since 2014-2015 (24%).[14] Compare this with another 44% who went online several times daily[15] and you have nearly nine-in-ten teens online a lot of their day—and that was 2018 (notice, however, that it doesn't say how long this latter group spends each time they go on, whether just a few minutes or hours at a time, though given the data that follows we can probably safely guess which is more likely). As for how often adults go online, a 2021 poll indicated 85% do at least daily—of these, 31% are on "almost constantly" (up from 21% in 2015), 48% several times daily, while a mere 6% go on once daily, and 7% never do.[16] Of those who report being online "almost constantly," 48% of these are 18-49-year-olds (up 9% since 2018 for those 18-29, and up 14% since 2015 among those 30-49), as compared to just 22% of those 50-64 (up from 12% since 2015), and only 8% of those 65 and older (unchanged since 2015).[17]

What about social media? Although 72% of Americans say they use it, in light of the numbers so far it probably won't surprise you to learn that those age 18-29, 30-49, and 50-64 are considerably more likely (84%, 81%, and 73%, respectively) to use it than those 65 and older (45%)—yet the use of these platforms by the last group has shot up sharply (181%) since 2012, as have the two categories beneath it (age 30-49: up 27%; age 50-64: up 87%).[18] And as with the stats for smartphone ownership, the percentage gap separating the youngest and oldest categories here has also greatly decreased, from 65 points in 2012 to 39 in 2021.[19] Two other unsurprising but notable aspects regarding this usage also stand out: the substantial percentage gap separating the youngest and oldest groups when it comes to which platforms each use (six of the most popular being YouTube, Facebook, Instagram, Snapchat, Twitter, and TikTok),[20] and the fact that for each of these age categories the percentage of users of each platform consistently decreases from youngest to oldest, especially on those other than YouTube and Facebook, which remain the most popular among adults overall, while Instagram, Snapchat, and TikTok are the three most popular among 18-29-year-olds (though they also use YouTube and Facebook as much as, or more than, the older groups).[21] As of 2022, teens also continue mostly to prefer the above platforms (especially TikTok, 67%), with the notable exception of Facebook (teen use has plummeted 39 points to 32% since 2014-2015).[22] More concerning, however, is the finding that roughly one in five teens use the above platforms (except Facebook) "almost constantly."[23]

Of course, both teens and adults also regularly use many other popular platforms, but these stats at least provide a basic picture of just how preoccupied people have become in this respect alone. And while there are lots of other fascinating demographic breakdowns as to the use of smartphones and social media, they are superfluous to my point here. However, in light of how politically divided Americans have become over the last decade, it was amusing to notice that, with the exception of two platforms, Democrats and Republicans are actually united in the similarity of the social media they use, especially Facebook.[24] I'm sure I'll sleep better knowing that.

But while these stats help to paint a slightly more nuanced picture of our present situation, their significance is substantially diminished in the absence of further data revealing some of their actual consequences (beyond my own sub-clinical observations). Before we go there, however, a quick point of clarification should be made regarding the data just mentioned. While the particular cutoff points distinguishing the generational groupings (e.g. 18-29, etc.) are not arbitrary, with the exception of the oldest two groups their parameters are not so firmly established that they might not change down the road as researchers continue to collect data.[25] That said, their differences are still critically meaningful and have something to say about the political, economic, and social factors that have affected, and continue to affect, the formative years of those within each category. These groups are often referred to by their familiar nicknames, distinguished by the range of their birth year: Silents (1928-1945), Baby Boomers (1946-1964), Gen X (1965-1980), and Millennials (1981-1996),[26] though with respect to the Pew data cited there is some overlap between them, since most of these sources organized their data according to the age groupings at the time of the study rather than by birth-year category, which means the makeup of each of these varies with each citation depending upon the year each survey was taken. But you might have noticed that the youngest category, referred to thus far as "teens," is conspicuously missing, which is because researchers are not yet entirely agreed as to what to call them—however, Pew analysis of Google Trends in 2019 revealed that the term Gen Z (born after 1996)[27, 28] is currently the most popular term (over *iGen* or *Post-Millennial*).[29] And while each of these generational groups have been impacted in unique ways by the different forms of technology, or lack thereof, prominent during their respective generations—Boomers by television, Gen Xers by the personal computer, and Millennials by the dawn of the internet—this Gen Z cohort, like it or not, will be the first from the cradle onward to grow up taking for granted not just all three of these substantial technological breakthroughs, but also the smartphone and social media.[30] Which factor by itself, of course, for better and for worse, will impact them much differently than every generational subgroup before them. With regard to this generation one writer was so bold as to comment, "It's not an exaggeration to describe iGen as being on the brink of the worst mental-health crisis in decades. Much of this deterioration can be traced to their phones."[31] Abigail Shrier, best-selling author of the devastating exposé, *Irreversible Damage*, echoes this assessment:

> If I had told you in 2007 that one device would produce a sudden skyrocketing in self-harm among teens and tweens, you would likely have said, "No way is my kid getting one." And yet, here we are: the statistical explosion of bullying, cutting, anorexia, depression, and the rise of sudden transgender identification is owed to the

self-harm instruction, manipulation, abuse, and relent-
less harassment supplied by a single smartphone.[32]

But the potential consequences of all this overexposure to
touchscreen technology don't apply only to Gen Z. Unfortunately,
there's plenty of crisis to go around. Consider what researchers at
the University of Pennsylvania found in 2018, in a study published
in the *Journal of Social and Clinical Psychology*, in which they asked
143 undergraduates either to limit their use of Facebook, Snapchat, and Instagram to ten minutes, per platform, per day, for
three weeks, or to continue using social media as they normally
would.[33] Three weeks later, the participants in the former group
reported less depression, loneliness, and anxiety, not to mention
diminished feelings of an increasingly common phenomenon referred to as FOMO—Fear of Missing Out.[34] In the same year, an
online article in *Forbes* spoke of similar findings: "Plenty of studies have found correlations between higher social media use and
poorer mental health, including depression, anxiety, feelings of
loneliness and isolation, lower self-esteem, and even suicidal-
ity."[35] One such study, done in 2017 at the University of Pittsburgh
and published in the *American Journal of Preventative Medicine*,
found that people age 19 to 32 who used social media for more
than two hours per day were twice as likely to experience social
isolation than those who spent less than half an hour—"Participants who visited various social media platforms 58 or more
times per week had about triple the odds of feeling socially isolated than those who visited fewer than nine times per week."[36]
Another study published in the same journal in 2020 by researchers from the University of Arkansas revealed that adults between
18 and 30 who spent five hours or more per day on social media
were almost three times as likely to develop depression as those
who only spent two hours or less per day.[37] Likewise, a professor

and researcher at San Diego State University who found a correlation between the increase of smartphone usage among teens and a decrease in their psychological well-being advises, "Aim to spend no more than two hours a day on social media, and try to increase the amount of time you spend seeing friends face-to-face and exercising—two activities reliably linked to greater happiness."[38]

Finally, a few other eye-opening facts in this regard are also worth pondering. In 2018 the AAA Foundation for Traffic Safety found that texting while driving doubles the chances of a car accident, and the Virginia Tech Transportation Institute says you are six times more likely to crash while texting and driving than if you are driving drunk.[39] Is it any wonder, then, that 48 states have already banned this egregious behavior? Another study done recently by a team of researchers at the University of California, San Diego, found that the overall rate of cell phone-related injury for children under 21—those reported as emergency room visits, grouped by age: 0-2; 3-10; 11-15; 16-18; 19-21—increased from 17.1 injuries per 100,000 in 2002 to 138 in 2015, an increase of 707% (if you can believe it, the greatest increase by age-category was the 3-10 group at 705%, while the smallest was the 19-21 group at 634%).[40, 41]

Even if these last data alone were the sole measure of the extent of the quandary in which we find ourselves, are they not sufficient to give us pause?

Sometimes when reminiscing about the old days in comparison to these recent trends, some of my old classmates and I mutually acknowledge how thankful we are to have grown up the way we did, knowing no different. Despite how bored we sometimes were back then, sprawled out on the same couch without a thing to do but stare idly into space, chatting about nothing of practical importance, still we remained directly engaged with one another. Lacking the seductive, portable technology kids take for granted nowadays, we were able to share more than simply space and time, as opposed to what seems like the new normal among young people lately, though not just Gen Z: the nonstop navel-gazing narcissism that keeps their attention fixed primarily on their phones, and only secondarily on one another, as they mindlessly murmur back and forth.

I'm thankful I never (ever) worry about my battery running out or feel the need to bring a charger with me everywhere I go. I can't relate to so many I see who are constantly plugged into an outlet wherever they find one, even in public. I'm thankful that the compulsions so many nowadays not only feel but seem unable, or unwilling, to resist are largely foreign to me. I'm thankful to be able to hear the multiple notification chimes sound off at any given time of day and not feel the obligation to respond on cue like some kind of Pavlovian mutt. Although it's worth remembering, and humbling to contemplate, that this might not be the case, or as much so, if I hadn't been born and raised at the particular time and place that I was, or by the same parents—which is to say if factors beyond my control were not mostly, if not exactly, what by the grace of God they just so happened to be.

And yet I'm flesh and blood like anyone else, far from immune to overreliance on and overuse of the latest touchscreen technology and apps. What I find both surprising and not so surprising is how even a person like myself who didn't grow up with these and lived most of my adult life without them—I managed to hold out until 2015 before buying my first smartphone—can still experience the uneasy feeling of having forgotten something whenever I go anywhere without it, which almost never happens anymore.

And that feeling, of course, is a feeling of anxiety, however short-lived or shallowly felt. And if it's this way for someone so disconnected, so indifferent to the thing, however useful it can be, it's easier to imagine what it might feel like for those more deeply dialed in. If for some reason tomorrow I had to go back to slowly scrawling out paper reminders on the kitchen table, I have to say I would not only be disappointed, I would whine audibly, finding it much less convenient, efficient, and effective than their digital alternative, which helps me immeasurably every single day, wherever I happen to be. This is mostly, though not only, on account of the voice-to-text means of making these notes and reminders, another priceless blessing—especially for a writer and quadriplegic who happens to be physically unable to use a flip-phone, and who only with equal parts concentration and frustration is able to slowly knuckle-type short phrases on the puny keyboard of a smartphone. And while the portability of the device is another integral part of its convenience and effectiveness, ironically this is part of what makes it so vexing for those of us who are conscious of the degree to which we tend to depend on them. Everywhere we go we are challenged to restrain our impulses, from gaming to general web surfing to social media to simply talking or texting. This mindset recognizes that there is a time and place for each of these, just not anytime and everywhere we feel like it, without asking ourselves where and when and to what degree this is appropriate. And as usual it's no surprise to discover that our curiosity is a large part of our problem, which too often includes the need to know right this minute even the most mundane and unnecessary details when a nano-speck of patience might not kill us on the spot. In fact, I have to laugh at myself sometimes as I anxiously murmur, *Come on, come on*, to a webpage or other document that is taking more than five whole seconds to load. I have to scold myself, tell myself to chill out, remember what it was like twenty years ago listening to the fax-like death-screech of the dial-up modem and how it wasn't unusual to wait several minutes even for basic images, forget about videos, to load. It's moments like these when I mock myself as a hopeless child of this age.

I can still remember the awe of setting eyes for the first time on a touchscreen, a first-generation (Apple) iPad, circa 2010. Having never seen up close any of the early forerunners to such a device, the very concept of a touchscreen was as mind-blowing as mesmerizing even to imagine, let alone see and feel. By *feel* I don't so much mean the physical sensation but rather the apparent miracle of a colorful, high-resolution glass surface instantly responding to the delicacy of your horizontal and vertical finger (or in my case knuckle) swipes, the fine touch required to make it work (that is, it won't if you push too lightly or too long). Which strangely enables you to feel a kind of interconnectedness with the device in a way previously unknown. Likewise, when in due time an updated model made it possible to zoom in or out on either text or pictures simply by pinching with your thumb and forefinger, it carried away your astonishment to yet another level (another feature that even my clumsy knuckles, with both hands working together, are able to pull off).

This level of technology is obviously the kind of breakthrough that only comes along once in a blue moon, at least as much of a game-changer as the dawn of the television, personal computer, internet, or cellular revolution. And just think how quickly that awe at the unimaginable, what we lived without for so long, wears off, as it always does for us sooner than later, no matter what the new discovery happens to be. There is always a honeymoon period when, flattered by our own collective genius as a race, we glory in the innovation, often at the cost of conveniently ignoring or downplaying any less-than-positive implications. Drunk on our own pride, ingenuity, ambition, and momentum, we charge full speed ahead until, as always, wouldn't you know, the newfangled gadget becomes old hat, ho hum, what's next? It's been more than a decade now that we've had the touchscreen, so you might think people would have had their fill by now, especially those who have used it the longest. But as with the personal computer, especially when you factor in the internet, there is such a plentiful supply of things both pointless and useful to do and learn that it's no wonder the spell hasn't worn off yet, and probably never will at the rate we are going with so many new developments daily flooding the scene. In fact, at this point it seems like the only thing capable of spoiling this craze is either an autocratic government edict or prolonged, universal blackouts.

I sometimes try to imagine what might happen—though doubtless it already has—if some brave soul wandered into the heart of some remote, primitive tribe and demonstrated even some of the more rudimentary capabilities of the latest touchscreen device. Can you see them standing there half-naked, staring and pointing and possibly laughing at the crazy outsider who has so lost his marbles that he is actually speaking to the lifeless object in his hand as if it were his friend? Then, a moment later, the confused horror on their faces as they clutch onto one another, hearing the bizarre foreign object instantaneously reply, in fact in their own unique dialect (don't worry, if we're not quite there yet, we will be before you know it). Presumably their response would be prompt one way or the other: either to slay the wicked messenger, undoubtedly a powerful witch doctor, or else to collapse at his feet in worship, mistaking him for God. In the latter case, imagine the outsider leaving each of his new admirers a device of their own, then returning a year later to find their humble way of life radically disfigured, everyone lying about lazily for hours at a time with their stupefied gazes brightly lit up by a most unnatural form of light.

To be sure, anyone who has used a cell phone—especially a smartphone—with any realistic consistency will likely be slow to deny how practically useful they can be in seemingly endless ways. This is especially true with respect to emergencies, which used to be people's number one and often only reason for getting one in the first place—to have on hand, just in case. Remember that? I'm old enough to remember hearing this justification all the time not so long ago: I *need* one. That was always the operative language, especially among the post-forty crowd, as though they had to persuade you for permission. This self-induced confession seemed subtly to imply a sense of guilt or shame associated with the desire. But why would that be? Embarrassed at the thought of trusting a device in an emergency rather than, say, the general be-nevolence of strangers, or God? (By the way, anytime you find yourself justifying your actions to anyone, especially to yourself, pay attention—this is more often than not your default self-preservation software kicking in to assuage your conscience.) And that was *before* the smartphone, when landlines were the sta-tus quo, when the sight of someone using even a flip-phone or BlackBerry (remember those?) caused him to be looked upon with surprise, or even suspicion or contempt, as if to say: *Look at you, Mr. Big Shot, with your fancy, high-tech gizmo.* Not that this was drastically overt, but at the time cell phone users were a dis-tinct minority, not to mention the fact that most of us—even those who have never seen *2001: A Space Odyssey*—have an inbuilt and often warranted skepticism toward sudden (or sometimes even gradual) changes to how we are accustomed to doing things, es-pecially when it comes to new technology. At any rate, with the exception of parents, you don't hear people justifying themselves this way anymore, which is probably because there are now plenty of other practical reasons for the average adult to justify their *need* for one—a smartphone, that is, which is something like the twenty-first century version of a Swiss Army knife, only cooler and more sophisticated, a very handy and powerful thing indeed to have in your pocket or purse. As compared to a flip-phone, that is, which despite its few remaining admirers may be driven into extinction sooner than you think.[42, 43] The other reason few people feel compelled to justify themselves this way anymore is because this stigma is no more, meaning you are no longer in the lonesome, suspect minority now if you happen to want or *need* one.

But before moving on, let's come back to parents for a moment, among whom it has become increasingly common to hear the same sort of justifications just mentioned—in fact, the same language—in this case for the sake of their kids: their *need* to keep track of them via cell phone when they are out and about, unsupervised or otherwise, in case of emergency (never mind how many generations before them, even in America, even just a decade ago, somehow managed without, as multitudes worldwide still seem to). But here the justifications for this *need* are slightly different from those just mentioned. If in a similar way this apparent self-defense maneuver implies a feeling of guilt or shame, in this case, since the stigma mentioned above is no more, it either has to do with the fact just mentioned, that there is an awareness that the phones-for-kids-policy is ultimately unnecessary, or else with the recognition that the phones being provided are often not just the basic flip-phones, which every parent knows are more than sufficient to serve the purpose, but the smartphone, for which there is apparently a special need, whether this comes at the behest of the parents or the kids (can't you just hear the latter begging for the one over the other, exploiting the time-tested childhood bargaining chip: *all my friends have them*?). Meanwhile, kids of all ages everywhere are becoming accustomed to this often unrestricted, twenty-four-seven online access and all its potential, for better and for worse. Even when parents have the wisdom to set boundaries on such access, kids often discover clever ways around them, which means the number of influences they are exposed to—tons of them unthinkably horrendous—suddenly increases exponentially. Like it or not, parents, there is a trade-off you make when you allow your kids to have a smartphone: potential security and convenience now in exchange for potentially detrimental psycho-social side effects and habits both now and down the road. And it's not like parents are unaware of this. A Pew survey from 2020 found that 71% of parents believe pervasive use of smartphones by children under twelve might potentially lead to more harm than benefits, including their ability to learn effective social skills.[44] But you have to wonder how many among this percentage still allow their kids to have them, with or without restrictions. Isn't it disconcerting enough that only 71% of the respondents believe this? Or the fact that 68% of these parents admitted they are at least sometimes—and 17% often—distracted by their *own* phone when spending time with their kids?[45] It's at least somewhat comforting to learn that 86% of those interviewed limit the length of time, or the time of day, their children under twelve can use screens.[46] But if nothing else convinces you how drastically different these current trends are from just ten and twenty years ago, consider that 80% of the above respondents report taking away their child's smartphone or internet privileges as a form of "digital discipline."[47]

But what if we ask what lies behind these habitual, often obsessive-compulsive tendencies? Do we really need a PhD to figure this out? We have mentioned the obvious usefulness and convenience of these devices, including the fact that people enjoy using them, whatever their reasons, which may be as simple as relieving boredom or as practical as connecting with family and friends or using GPS to navigate your travels. And it's probably not too unreasonable to suggest that for many this is just the latest and easiest means of escape, the consequences of which are not all immediately evident, but in some cases may only appear later, therefore the general reluctance of most to acknowledge the potential dangers. But are the above reasons alone sufficient to account for their broad and intoxicating appeal?

Whatever other factors are to blame, one in particular is undeniably central for multitudes, though by and large ignored, even by—or perhaps especially by—those who are its most unwitting victims. Like most console-based video game systems, which are becoming more and more immersive and lifelike every year, many games for the smartphone—even the less-sophisticated ones—as well as the most popular social media platforms, are also designed with the addiction of their users in mind. This is an astounding open secret that most people shrug off like it's no big deal, old news, we know this. But does this not seem predatory, in fact eerily similar to the means and motives of Big Tobacco and Big Pharma, whose primary concern, always and forever, like so many other multibillion-dollar industries, is not for the health and welfare of their customers, but rather for their exploitation as they seek to maximize their dividends? And what better business model to ensure the retainment (one might say enslavement) of your customer base than to get them physiologically hooked on your product? Of course, Big Tobacco accomplishes this via the portable, handheld devices with which we are all so familiar. Yet surprisingly it turns out that so does Big Tech. Their respective delivery devices may differ drastically in appearance and sophistication, but they both stimulate the same drug they use to their advantage. The former stimulates this delivery via the drug with which we are also very familiar, namely nicotine, whereas the latter does so by means of another, ostensibly less threatening one: video games and social media. And what drug are both of these designed to stimulate? Dopamine, of course, the so-called "happy hormone."

But is it fair to compare cigarettes to smartphones? Are not the former much more hazardous to one's health? This, of course, depends on how you define *hazardous* and *health*. The disastrous effects of smoking are now well-known and beyond dispute, and only the ignorant and reckless persist in doing so at great risk to their own, and sometimes others', well-being. But we are only just beginning to scratch the surface of the negative consequences of our excessive devotion to all this new technology, and yet in spite of what we already know, the pioneering masses plunge fearlessly forward into the abyss of the unknown. One thing we do know is that with social media and video games this conditioning happens just as subtly as with cigarettes, though in this case through a process social scientists call "variable-ratio reinforcement"—remember B. F. Skinner and his lever-pressing rats and pigeons?—a term which describes a "schedule" of behavioral reinforcement in which a response to a given stimulus is rewarded after an unpredictable number of responses. And wouldn't you know this just happens to be the most effective among several similar methods of behavior modification to ensure the longest-lasting commitment of its subjects,[48] which I suppose we are expected to believe is sheer coincidence. For example, your average Facebook or TikTok junkie, who regularly exposes herself to an almost constant onslaught of new posts and other information, will feel occasional doses of satisfaction (i.e. dopamine hits) each time a new or certain type of stimuli appears, or whenever her posts or comments are shown positive attention or "liked." In this way she isn't as different as she might think from those oblivious lab animals, or from the typical jackpot junkie repeatedly pulling the slot-machine lever in the veiled hope of feeling the same kind of occasional buzz. Which is in some part due to the fact that many social media platforms use predictive algorithms to anticipate and respond accordingly to the unique interests of users. Moreover, have you never wondered why the aptly named "feeds" of the most popular social media platforms are designed so as to allow you to scroll down endlessly? Should we really be so surprised to learn of studies with titles like "Brain anatomy alterations associated with Social Networking Site (SNS) addiction"?[49]

But despite the collective weight of all that has been said thus far, it wouldn't be unreasonable for someone to point out that it's no less virtuous to be excessively preoccupied by a smartphone than it is by a book or anything else. Obviously a person can be just as engrossed, and therefore just as distracted from his immediate surroundings, by a magazine or yo-yo as he can by a smartphone. But the main thrust of the argument thus far isn't so much about the rightness or wrongness of the act in itself—not taking into consideration the purpose for which the device is being used, or the particular content being consumed—as it is about the bigger picture. The central point here is the relatively sudden and steadily increasing dominance—in the U. S. and most everywhere, even right here in the Heartland—of smartphones over nearly every other form of occupying oneself, privately or publicly, and the general reluctance of most people to spend *any* of their spare waking minutes without being thus preoccupied, even when the preliminary data may warn of certain dangers in this respect. In fact, to witness someone without an earpiece in their ear or face fixed on their phone, or both, and therefore undistracted from the beauty of the birds and blue sky and other breathing beings immediately around them, even while out on a leisurely walk, is becoming a rare enough sight to make that person actually stand out, and to make you almost do a double-take, as if you've spotted an endangered species—and sadly it's quite possible you have. What was once the norm has quickly become the exception, and the exception the norm. As with so many other things, the purpose for which this innovation was initially created, presumably to help improve our ability to connect and communicate with one another, has morphed into something beyond what anyone probably expected in the beginning and has ironically become the very thing which causes so many to isolate themselves from one another. It's one thing for the negative implications of such excessive preoccupation to affect individuals in private, but when these habits are brought with increasing frequency into the public sphere where we interact with our fellow community members, however familiar or unfamiliar we are with them, they inevitably affect, and in many cases disrupt, the nature of our collective intercourse, which ultimately determines the overall cohesiveness of society as a whole, both locally and beyond.

And unfortunately, since the present status quo never proves to be quite enough in this audacious new age of seemingly endless and ubiquitous information and technological novelty, something inevitably comes along sooner than later and takes things up yet another notch. As happened fairly nonchalantly just before the end of 2021, when the behemoth formerly known as Facebook, Inc. announced that it was officially changing its name to Meta Platforms, Inc.—a fairly innocuous change, it seemed, until news began to spread like wildfire that thousands have already begun stumbling over one another to dish out ludicrous sums for virtual real estate within this pixelated landscape (a.k.a. the metaverse). That's right, digital property—described in one article as "computer-generated, networked extended reality, or XR, an acronym that embraces all aspects of augmented reality, mixed reality and virtual reality (AR, MR and VR)"[50]—by means of which entrepreneurs and investors are aiming to cash in big time in the coming years, a quasi-fictitious fantasy world in which its creators and proponents expect multitudes to spend a good bulk of their free time and money the same way they do now, only in a more immersive way, where they can live a kind of parallel existence, presumably achieving things impossible this side of reality, being whoever they want to be and doing whatever they want to do— as if there's not already enough of that happening in actual reality. And the honeymoon season is well underway, the romance of the masses being wooed by the siren song of what they've never experienced in quite the same way, and only the world's biggest fuddy-duddies will be unable to appreciate how hip and next-level it is.

In one sense you wonder if you can really say you are *actually* doing a thing if it's a *virtual* experience. On the other hand, while the reviews of alleged experts in this regard are many and mixed about what this metaverse will look like in five to fifteen years, including to what degree it will have positive or negative implications for mankind, it's all but certain to those that think they know a thing or two about it that the future will be composed of some mixture of reality and virtual reality, whether we're ready for it or not. As for its positive uses, it isn't hard to imagine its potential for removing danger from the training of certain high-risk professions like surgeons or soldiers or astronauts, or even perhaps the interactions of world leaders, who, due to a global pandemic or high-stakes political standoff, may occasionally need, if only temporarily, to "gather" virtually rather than face-to-face. As for the other side of the coin, consider a couple less-optimistic predictions, which one talking head describes as "the new frontier of surveillance capitalism," and another as "easier addiction to all-absorbing games and fantasy experiences resulting in increased isolation for many; further breakdown of social cohesion as the virtual offers an easy alternative to the hard task of learning to live with each other."[51]

However the metaverse ends up affecting mankind, the very existence of such a realm, and especially the cheerful and persistent promotion thereof before we have any realistic sense of what its implications might be on top of everything else, makes you wonder if people have forgotten that life is breathtakingly short the way it is—like a vapor, the Bible says—and therefore to squander any of it, let alone much of it, on a plane that doesn't really count in the grand scheme of things seems unwise, if only because it shortens what's left of that which is far from virtual, which does very much count. And if the prospect of the virtual realm were not by itself enough to give us reasonable cause for alarm as far as its potential to further entice the attention and affections of the masses—especially our children, who are, after all, the future—another even more recent breakthrough definitely should. That is, the power and potential of so-called "artificial intelligence," or AI, platforms, which already appear to be the up-and-coming replacement for the "search engines" on which we have so quickly and recently come to rely—the difference between the two being that, similar to Siri and Alexa, these newcomers on the scene function more like personalities, interacting with their curious, intrigued admirers in real-time back-and-forth exchanges to provide instantaneous responses to an endless variety of spontaneous, sometimes complex requests, like "Write me a two thousand-word essay on the chief causes of the fall of the Roman Empire," or "Is it ever ethical to lie or cheat or steal?" And regardless of how accurate or ethical its responses, they are provided as immediately as through the other artificial genies just mentioned (though slightly less so with more elaborate requests), which is to say faster than any human being could even think of providing them. More than that, these answers are almost always far more robust than those provided by the other entities, as line by line, paragraph by paragraph, the blank page before you is spontaneously populated with an alarmingly coherent compilation of ideas attempting to meet your unique request, in some cases incorporating information from earlier in the conversation to do so. Thus, the novel thrill of such interactions, which are surprisingly not unlike our conversations with actual human beings, can leave one with the feeling of having discovered an extremely fascinating and resourceful new friend—and without any apparent downside, except perhaps making us even more lazy and dependent than usual on technology to do our research and thinking for us.

But while your immediate gratifications are being satisfied, your clever pal is learning from these interactions in ways and on levels that you are not, including how to avoid in the future any mistakes it may have made, thereby making it wiser and more powerful, which is evidently now possible for machines, which aren't prone to forget like we do. More troubling than that, there is every reason to believe that your new friend is also learning about you in particular, the unique idiosyncrasies that characterize how and on what level you think and interact, perhaps sizing you up so as to determine how best to engage with you in order to achieve certain objectives, possibly to change your mind and use you for its own ends, be they political or commercial. If that sounds paranoid—especially when you think of your kids using it—you might ask yourself if you really believe that entities like this, including Siri and Alexa, have been made so widely and easily accessible simply to make your life more convenient. Questions like this are part of the reason why there is already substantial, widespread concern and debate over where all this is headed, including what the implications might be if such technology breaks free from the constraints with which it was initially designed (hmm, sounds like a familiar story). There have even been calls recently by certain prominent figures of the tech world for a six-month moratorium on the development of such platforms so that experts in the field can more seriously assess and troubleshoot some of the more potentially hazardous scenarios that could crop up. And if that's not an indication that just maybe this time we might be in a little over our heads, I'm not sure what it's going to take to get our attention.

And while this aspect of the conversation may seem like a digression, its importance and centrality to the overall theme is obvious when you remember that the parameters for how these frighteningly intelligent entities gather, track, and analyze information have been set and are very likely being constantly manipulated by anonymous human beings employed by multinational corporations who have their own particular worldviews and prerogatives—which, of course, inevitably shape the way in which information can and can't be accessed, including in what light it is portrayed as far as whether or not it is deemed appropriate for public consumption. Thus, the recent increase in the use of terms like "misinformation" and "disinformation" by governments and legacy media are clear warning signs of their attempt to sway the public discourse in their favor. Which makes you wonder if these social engineers are acting in ignorance of or adherence to the dystopian classics of literature that were intended as warnings, rather than as manuals for emulation.

At any rate, while it does arouse some hope to learn that the older Internet users are the less likely they are to view it as a positive for society, that hope is quickly dashed when the same poll also reveals that the approval levels of the eldest three groups—all of whom grew up without the internet and cellular-touchscreen technology—are higher than you might expect: Gen

X 69%, Boomers 68%, Silents 63%.[52] This, of course, means that the ones who have been around the longest, and therefore have the most life experience in general, including the advantage of having lived both with and without these technologies, still more or less consider their effect on society positive. And since in many cases the younger, greater multitude accustomed to keeping themselves so preoccupied, virtually or otherwise, do so because it's been the norm for them practically since they were in diapers, our hope for the future in this regard sags further yet.

In the temporary absence of hope, however, as if to offer their own plea to our present state of affairs, a handful of random, pop-culture soundbites suddenly volunteer themselves. First, an old lyric by '90s popstar Alanis Morrissette: "Why are you so petrified of silence?"[53] Except in this case we might ask: *Why are you so petrified of being unoccupied?* Then a classic line from one of the most iconic cinematic personas of the '80s, Ferris Buehler, a sage for the modern age: "Life moves pretty fast—you don't stop and look around once in a while, you could miss it."[54] Lastly, going back a little before my time, a few selected lines from an old song by *The Association*[55] that inspired the title of this essay (go ahead and google it to hear the tune and sing along):

> I took off my watch [I want to say instead: *I put down my phone*]
> Found I had all the time in the world
> I opened my arms, so I could hold life like a beautiful girl
> I laid down all of my hangups forever
>
> I looked around and saw what sweet things can be found
> Simply by taking some time for livin'
> Groovin' on the little things that life is givin'
> From now on I'm takin' time for life
>
> Too busy to stop and notice the things that are real

Embarrassed to talk about all the things I feel
It's so strange, never noticed all the world around me

As the above lines vividly highlight, even without all this ex-cess preoccupation with the latest technology, it's easy enough to get caught up in the hustle-bustle-rat-race of life, simply going through the mechanical motions of weekly routines like drones, taking for granted nearly everything, including life itself, as if we've got all the time in the world to do whatever it is we are here to do. Besides affecting the nature of our personal interactions with one another, this persistently distracted lifestyle also inhib-its our ability to exercise one of our chief functions and gifts as "fearfully and wonderfully made" creatures: to contemplate our world on something more than the most superficial level. You would think people have forgotten that we need some free time now and then to reflect on life and all it entails, including the deeper, existential things like what we believe, and why, about how we got here in the first place and what comes after this—all of which requires the deliberate choice to resist the rat-race pace and mentality, to be still and unoccupied long enough to receive what life has to offer in its essential, organic, non-manufactured simplicity. Picture a child gazing into a cloudless sky and wonder-ing why it's blue. It hardly needs to be said that this meditative aspect of our existence is indispensable to our emotional and spir-itual well-being and actually transcends being in its most basic sense, where mere perception gives way to reflection, rumination, illumination, transformation. Thinking along different but similar lines, the late German philosopher Josef Pieper put it this way:

When we really let our minds rest contemplatively on a rose in bud, on a child at play, on a divine mystery, we are rested and quickened as though by a dreamless sleep ....

It is in these silent and receptive moments that the soul of man is sometimes visited by an awareness of what holds the world together.[56]

Even as an end in itself, for the simple pleasure of doing so, this basic act is worth taking time for, even when it serves no overt utilitarian end, as far as this workaday world is concerned. Of course, doing so is impossible when our attention is more or less constantly captivated by something else, a fact which seems lost on this present culture and age. If only the average hyper-distracted soul could be troubled to spare just a few precious minutes each day for this, who knows what the implications might be, both for himself and for the world around him? Even if by some miracle this did begin to happen with more regularity, we could also hope such souls might choose more noble objects of contemplation than what has been conceived and mass-produced by mere mortals.

But someone might object: *Am I not contemplating the things I'm looking at on my phone?* Allowing the benefit of the doubt, we are probably safe to assume there's at least enough going on between such a person's ears to distinguish him from a rock. But the real question in this case is not whether there's more going on than simple perception, but to what degree beyond that default surface level are most such folks operating, and for how long? If, as so often happens while you are reading something—even on your phone—you stop here and there to ponder a certain idea, if only for ten or twenty seconds, then maybe we could dare to call this contemplation, or more likely the beginning thereof. But if, as seems to be the case with so many smartphone users, you are not in the habit of permitting even such abbreviated interruptions, but instead are almost constantly inundated by a steady stream of stimuli that in most cases changes just as constantly, then we dare not mistake this for contemplation. We might compare this latter state of mind to that which prevails as you watch a movie—however closely you may try to keep pace with the dialogue, plot, directing style, or cinematography, if you stop very long to ponder any one of these, you miss out on the others, especially the story itself as it moves on without you. That is to say you are inhibited from fixing your concentrated meditation on a single subject long enough to gain some significant insight, as opposed to being a sounding board for what might be described as successive microbursts of fleeting titillation.

And while it's one thing to see this happening to adults, who have no excuse for not knowing any better, especially in the face of mounting evidence that such habits can be significantly destructive to self and society, it's another thing entirely to realize how much more serious this is with respect to children. Enabling them to carry on like this as a regular habit, often for extended periods at a time, disrupts and distracts the instinctive childhood process of inquiry and discovery that requires unimpeded room to explore what they think about the natural world and how to connect the dots in their own unique ways. Interrupt that sacred space and you allow for a substantial alteration to the naturally ordained course of things, breaking unprecedented ground historically and anthropologically. And if it's not bad enough that this is happening to kids at such early ages, and on so broad a scale, the crisis is further exacerbated by the fact that in most cases it continues unabated into adulthood. Parents, of course, bear much of the responsibility for this, but what about the rest of us as a collective whole, in keeping with the notion that it takes a village to raise a child?

Waiting rooms of any kind are one of the best places to notice the prevalence of people choosing their phones over any other form of preoccupation, because at any given time you have half a dozen to a dozen people clustered within a relatively small space, which tends to highlight the phenomenon more than when the same number of people are more widely dispersed in the great outdoors. And if I had to guestimate from my semi-scientific observations over the past decade, users typically outnumber non-users about five to one, among whom the under-forty, and especially under-twenty, crowd are the most likely offenders. The saddest sight to me is that of a parent and her child simultaneously captivated for long stretches by their respective touchscreens, almost completely incommunicado, which is in all likelihood a reasonable indicator that this is the norm when they are at home. Moreover, it's almost unheard of anymore to see someone bring their own book or crossword puzzle or knitting project, or just sit there, like me, silently looking on. In some cases you don't even see magazines on the end tables anymore, which I find a little discouraging, as if whoever is in charge of this, noticing the trend, finally gave up.

Having been surrounded for so many years by such a scenario, and not only in waiting rooms, I have resolved, with few exceptions, to stay off my phone in indoor public settings when there are others around. I still leave it sitting right out on my lap as always, though—available but neglected. If it dings, I ignore it. If it rings, I swipe to decline. My hope, however futile, has been to make people think twice when they see such a profound oddity, a breathing billboard for the almost inconceivable alternative of sitting quietly without being stimulated by anything other than your own thoughts. They'll never know that it's not as easy for me as it might look to sit there rereading the same uninteresting signs on patient rights (some of them in Spanish), staring at the same bland watercolor paintings or design schemes of the carpet, making occasional, accidental eye-contact as often as each one periodically glances up from their self-induced trance (sometimes I stare at them just long enough to make them look up, then quickly look away). Truth be told, I'd rather make the most of these spare minutes by studying my Greek New Testament—because, of course, there is an app for about everything—but I refuse in the hope that one day some courageous soul might dare to join me in swimming against the mighty current of the latest status quo (cue the hallelujah chorus).

None of this means to disparage how legitimately busy people are trying to run their businesses and households as efficiently as possible, and how helpful these devices can be in achieving that end, wherever a person may be. Besides, some who may at times appear to be engrossed with their phones in private or public may only do so briefly a few times the whole day, which is to say we all know the dangers of jumping to conclusions and judging too hastily. But let's conclude with a little agreement, shall we, mutually conceding that many people's behavior in this regard—sometimes even our own—has gotten a little out of control? Maybe a few straightforward questions wouldn't be out of line? Do you spend more time each day interacting with a smartphone than with other human beings—not counting the ones you connect with through the device, including for what your job requires? Are you able to last even five minutes before looking at or responding to notifications of any kind? Do you tend to panic or worry if your phone is in danger of losing power, or loses power, or its signal, and you have no way to charge or recover it? Do you have any hesitation about asking perfect strangers if you can use their Wi-Fi or charger? Are you so preoccupied with your phone that you sometimes stumble into people or objects (whether they are moving or stationary)? If one or more of these describe you, then it's probably time to consider making some changes in this regard. After all, there seems to be reason for hope.

At a recent doctor visit, only one of the nine people seated around me (a neighbor of mine) was using his cell phone—he was actually yammering away on speakerphone, which is fortunately rare in public indoor spaces. In fact, each of the others seemed quite content sitting there quietly like me, staring at something other than their hands, which almost made me wonder if I was dreaming or hallucinating or if my conclusions along these lines might need reevaluating (though in fairness I have only once since then witnessed a similar scene). It was also surprising to observe that the only other phone I noticed, another smartphone, was stuck in the external purse pocket of an elderly woman. And to be honest, though it may seem contrary to my purpose here, I always admire seeing folks this age operating smartphones, if only because in some ways they are not so easy to learn how to use, especially for older generations who are new to the concept of touchscreen technology, so I give them credit for trying—by which I don't mean to condescend or imply that those who prefer the simplicity of a flip-phone are any less sophisticated. I also appreciate the fact that those in this demographic are generally much less likely to be the ones exhibiting the various trends bemoaned thus far. And I have to say it was pretty odd, and not a little amusing, seeing everyone sit there unoccupied for once, trying their level best not to make eye-contact with one another as if we were all stuck in the same uncomfortable elevator. And though it may have only been an anomaly, a temporary glitch in the matrix, the more optimistic side of me would like to think it might represent a glimmer of hope for the future.

So where does all this leave us? Over a very short period of time, multitudes of Americans from every demographic have been gradually, very subtly conditioned to build their personal and professional lives and schedules around smartphones. In addition to offering virtually limitless potential for entertainment, these devices have become so useful and integral to nearly everything we do that, unless some drastic change occurs to our present way of life, they are not likely to be forsaken anytime soon. For these and other reasons, this general trend of collective preoccupation with them has been so quickly and uncritically welcomed as the latest and greatest status quo, having virtually sedated much of the populace into neglecting even the most superficial consideration of the potential short- and long-term effects of this on both themselves and the wider culture. What in most cases began as casual tendencies have quickly devolved into diehard habits, as yet one more Pew survey corroborates, revealing that while 54% of smartphone users in 2014 said their phone was "not always needed," just three years later 46% reported that their phone was something they couldn't live without.[57]

But if the predicament we seem to be in is as significant and multi-tentacled as our own observations and plentiful data seem to suggest, offering practical solutions isn't so simple and straightforward as recognizing the symptoms. Unless we are prepared to allow the state or federal government to step in and start passing more laws similar to those pertaining to driving—which in this case would stipulate how cell phones may and may not be used in other public spaces, or whether there should be age restrictions for smartphones or social media, in private or public—we must be satisfied to entrust any hope we may have for changes to these current trends and tendencies to rest solely in the will of the individual. After all, even if such formal restrictions were deemed necessary and feasible to enact, we almost shudder to ask how they might be monitored and enforced—cameras everywhere, indoors and out? Social credit scores for ratting out your neighbor? But if that option seems sufficiently dystopian to put off for the time being, then unfortunately we are left with our current policy, which essentially leaves each individual or family to do whatever seems right in their own eyes.

Which leaves us right back where we started, hoping that, if we haven't already passed the point of no return as a culture, we might be willing fairly soon here to start having a more serious collective conversation about practical, feasible mitigating measures to address what we should have no hesitation labeling a rampant epidemic—to start calling a spade a spade and face the music, even if it's playing Taps. Or are we too embarrassed to admit our almost universal culpability, and would rather save face and let things play out as they will? This isn't about getting rid of the technology or the devices, it's about stepping back for a moment to look in the mirror, to adjust our vision beyond our own personal standpoint for a change, which, granted, isn't exactly an easy ask from a society as self-absorbed as it is complacent. After all, this requires the discipline to look beyond the present moment of instant gratification long enough to contemplate what it means to live in what still remains a mostly free and civil society, the ultimate viability of which requires regular in-person interaction with one another—and not just a cold intermingling of bodies exchanging perfunctory nods and salutations, the bare minimum to maintain a mediocre utilitarian coexistence. No, the frayed threads of that way of life are not far from unraveling entirely. On the contrary, times of crisis call for conviction, courage, and sacrifice, all of which, sorry to say, seem to be in short supply these days, even if we were in the fortunate position of being at the stage of discussing together whether or not the present situation even constitutes a crisis. As it is, there seems to be a kind of unspoken consensus that having such a discussion is not just unpalatable, but unnecessary, and without this baby-step beginning, this necessary least common denominator of agreement, we can't take the second step of asking from everyone involved some degree of sacrifice—which is a sacrifice of self-interest—toward addressing this alleged crisis.

But suppose one day in neo-democratic America the powers that be should by some inexplicable stroke of serendipity finally come to their senses (or their wits' end) and surprise us by mandating a no-stone-left-unturned policy to this end—if only for a brief trial period—that compels every American adult and their household to examine the motives that lie behind how often and in what settings they use their mobile devices, both publicly and privately, including the presuppositions that feed these motives, so as to foster the making of some concessions and moderations of habit on a broad scale, for the sake of an ideal higher than each one's own appetites, what some might call the Greater Good, namely our future together as part of what we take for granted as a mostly cohesive aggregate living under the privilege of law and order and relative prosperity. Provided the "powers" in charge of such an experiment are not thoroughly autocratic in nature (which implies, at the very least, ubiquitous surveillance and substantial consequences imposed for every act of insubordination), one can imagine the potentially hopeful prospect of some degree of positive change in the right direction, namely toward more, rather than less, self-restraint in this regard. On the other, probably more-realistic hand, given so many signs of social disharmony and moral decadence already written all over the proverbial walls—including persistent and pervasive disobedience to the laws already in place in this respect (e.g. cell phone use while driving)—if the negative consequences of this techno-toxication are not instantly felt by the average user, and if the reward for making self-restricting sacrifices for the sake of neighbor and self is not immediately gratifying or otherwise appealing, how should we expect such a well-intentioned program to succeed? At any rate, whether the sustainability of our future together will be determined by Big Brother forcing us to change our ways, or by leaving matters in our own hands and letting the present state of things continue to run its course, we have no one to blame but ourselves. If only the happy-go-lucky words toward the end of that old tune mentioned earlier might find renewed appeal along these lines on a revolutionary scale:

> Hey, look, I've changed, my attitude's been rearranged
> From now on I'm takin' some time for livin'
> Groovin' on everythin' life is givin'
> I'm gonna be takin' time for life, for livin'

---

[1] Richard M. Weaver, *Ideas Have Consequences* (University of Chicago Press, Ltd. London, 2013), 2.

[2] The first became available in 1983, the Motorola DynaTAC 800x, from which the first ever cellular phone call was made in 1973.

[3] Erik Gregersen, "Martin Cooper," Encyclopedia Britannica, https://www .britannica.com/biography/Martin-Cooper, Accessed Jun. 3, 2022.

[4] Apparently the lesser-known and less-celebrated LG Prada actually came shortly before, in 2006, but the sturdy, user-friendly iPhone proved to be what sparked the revolution that has followed.

[5] C. Scott Brown, "The LG Prada was the first capacitive touchscreen, not the iPhone," Feb. 15, 2020, https://www.androidauthority.com/lg-prada-1080646/.

[6] A 2018 Pew survey found that 74% of adult Facebook users were not aware that the site collects information on their personal traits and interests for the sake of advertisers; just over half of these respondents said this makes them uncomfortable.

[7] John Gramlich, "10 facts about Americans and Facebook," Jun. 1, 2021, https://www.pewresearch.org/fact-tank/2021/06/01/facts-about-americans-and-facebook/.

[8] Pew Research Center, "Mobile Fact Sheet," Apr. 7, 2021, https://www.pewresearch.org/internet/fact-sheet/mobile/.

[9] Ibid.

[10] Michelle Faverio, "Share of those 65 and older who are tech users has grown in the past decade," Jan. 13, 2022, https://www.pewresearch.org/fact-tank/2022/01/13/share-of-those-65-and-older-who-are-tech-users-has-grown-in-the-past-decade/.

[11] Ibid.

[12] Ibid.

[13] Monica Anderson and Jingjing Jiang, "Teens, Social Media and Technology 2018," May 31, 2018, https://www.pewresearch.org/fact-tank/2019/08/23/most-u-s-teens-who-use-cellphones-do-it-to-pass-time-connect-with-others-learn-new-things/.

[14] Emily A. Vogels, Risa Gelles-Watnick, and David Masssarat, "Teens, Social Media and Technology 2022," Aug. 10, 2022, https://www.pewresearch.org/internet/2022/08/10/teens-social-media-and-technology-2022/.

[15] Monica Anderson and Jingjing Jiang. Ibid.

[16] Andrew Perrin and Sarah Atske, "About three-in-ten U. S. adults say they are 'almost constantly' online," Mar. 26, 2021, https://www.pewresearch.org/fact-tank/2021/03/26/about-three-in-ten-u-s-adults-say-they-are-almost-constantly-online/.

[17] Ibid.

[18] Michelle Faverio, Ibid.

[19] Ibid.

[20] Ibid.

[21] Brooke Auxier and Monica Anderson, "Social Media Use in 2021," Apr. 7, 2021, https://www.pewresearch.org/internet/2021/04/07/social-media-use-in-2021/.

[22] Emily A. Vogels, Risa Gelles-Watnick, and David Masssarat, Ibid.

[23] Ibid.

[24] John Gramlich, Ibid.

25 Michael Dimock, "Defining generations: Where Millennials end and Generation Z begins," Jan. 17, 2019, https://www.pewresearch.org/fact-tank /2019/01/17/where-millennials-end-and-generation-z-begins/.

26 Kim Parker and Ruth Igielnik, "On the Cusp of Adulthood and Facing an Unknown Future: What We Know about Generation Z So Far," May 14, 2020, https://www.pewresearch.org/social-trends/2020/05/14/on-the-cusp-of-adulthood-and-facing-an-uncertain-future-what-we-know-about-gen-z-so-far-2/.

27 According to Pew Research Center, "no chronological endpoint has been set for this group," as this will depend on future data. These birth-range categories can also be defined by the age-range of each as of 2020—Gen Z: age 8-23; Millennials: 25-40; Gen X: 41-56; Boomers: 57-75; Silents: 76-93.

28 Michael Dimock; Kim Parker and Ruth Igielnik, Ibid.

29 Michael Dimock, Ibid.

30 Michael Dimock, Ibid.

31 Jean Tweng, "Have Smartphones Destroyed a Generation?" *The Atlantic*, Sep. 2017, https://www.theatlantic.com/magazinearchive/2017/09/.

32 Abigail Shrier, *Irreversible Damage: The Transgender Craze Seducing Our Daughters* (Regnery Publishing, Washington D.C., 2021), 212.

33 Melissa G. Hunt, Rachel Marx, Courtney Lipson, and Jordyn Young, "No More FOMO: Limiting Social Media Decreases Loneliness and Depression," *Journal of Social and Clinical Psychology*, Vol. 37, No. 10, 2018, 751.

34 Ibid.

35 Alice G. Walton, "New Studies Show Just How Bad Social Media Is For Mental Health," *Forbes*. Nov. 16, 2018, https://www.forbes.com.

36 Lindsay Dodgson, "Spending more than 2 hours on social media per day could make you feel isolated," Mar. 8, 2017, *Independent*, https://www.in-dependent.co.uk/tech/spending-more-than-2-hours-on-social-media-per-day-could-make-you-feel-isolated-a7618701.html.

37 Maggie Whalen, "Time on Social Media: How Much Is Too Much?" Dec. 16, 2020, https://www.thedoctorwillseeyounow.com/content/emotional _health/art6291.html#:~:text=By%20keeping%20your%20social%20me-dia,limits%20for%20their%20own%20use.

[38] Wagner, Neil. "Worried about Kids' Time Online?" Jan. 31, 2018. https://www.thedoctorwillseeyounow.com/content/kids/art5489.html.

[39] Drive Safe Online, "12 Important Texting and Driving Statistics," Oct. 1, 2020, https://www.drivesafeonline.org/defensive-driving/12-important-texting-and-driving-statistics/.

[40] Peter W. Guyon, Jr., Jamie Coroon, Karen Farran, Kathryn Hollenbach, and Margaret Nguyen, "Hold the Phone! Cell Phone-Related Injuries in Children, Teens, and Young Adults Are on the Rise," Oct. 28, 2020, National Library of Medicine, https://www.ncbi.nlm.nih.gov/pmc/articles /PMC7597570/.

[41] The bulk of these injuries, especially those in the oldest three groups, are related mainly to distracted mobility while doing other activities like walking or biking. And while the specifics behind these numbers are fascinating and tempting to include, their omission is due to the fact that the point is sufficiently made without them.

[42] By comparison, the BlackBerry, launched in 1999, became officially obsolete on January 4, 2022, a pretty good run for how simple it was.

[43] History Computer, "BlackBerry: Complete Guide – History, Products, Founding, and More," Jan. 31, 2022, https://www.history-computer.com /blackberry-history/.

[44] Brooke Auxier, Monica Anderson, Andrew Perrin, and Erica Turner, "Parenting Children in the Age of Screens," Jul. 28, 2020, https://www.pewresearch.org/internet/2020/07/28/parenting-children-in-the-age-of-screens/.

[45] Ibid.

[46] Ibid.

[47] Ibid.

[48] Saul McLeod, "What Is Operant Conditioning and How Does It Work?" Simply Psychology, 2018, https://www.simplypsychology.org/operant-conditioning.html#:~:text=Skinner%20found%20that%20the%20typeof %20extinction%20is%20continuous%20reinforcement.

[49] Qinghua He, Ofir Turel, and Antoine Bechara, "Brain anatomy alterations associated with Social Networking Site (SNS) addiction," Mar. 23, 2017, National Library of Medicine, https://www.ncbi.nlm.nih.gov/pmc/articles/PMC5362930/.

[50] Janna Anderson and Lee Rainie, "The Metaverse in 2040," Jun. 30, 2022, https://www.pewresearch.org/internet/2022/06/30/the-metaverse-in-2040/.

[51] Ibid.

[52] Emily A. Vogels, "Millennials stand out for their technology use, but older generations also embrace digital life," Sep. 9, 2019, https://www.pewresearch.org/fact-tank/2019/09/09/us-generations-technology-use/.

[53] Alanis Morissette, Glen Ballard, *All I Really Want*, (Album: Jagged Little Pill, 1995. Lyrics © Universal Music Publishing Group, Concord Music Publishing, LLC).

[54] Paramount Pictures presents a John Hughes film; produced by John Hughes and Tom Jacobson; written and directed by John Hughes, *Ferris Bueller's Day Off*, Hollywood, CA: Paramount Pictures Corp., 1986.

[55] Richard P. Addrisi, Donald J. Addrisi, *Time for Livin'* (Artist: The Association, 1968. Lyrics © Warner Chappell Music, Inc.).

[56] Pieper, Josef, *Leisure: The Basis of Culture*, trans. Alexander Dru (San Francisco: Ignatius Press, 2009), 47.

[57] Andrew Perrin, "10 facts about smartphones as the iPhone turns 10," Jun. 28, 2017, https://www.pewresearch.org/fact-tank/2017/06/28/10-facts-about-smartphones/.

Unleashed

Several years ago a colleague of mine mentioned a smartphone app that allows her to track the location of her boys (including her husband, who apparently tracks her the same way). Her sons were under ten at the time, though I have no doubt that this arrangement continues now that they are teenagers. As in so many cases, they have the phones in case of emergency, which is really to say in case my friend needs to get a hold of them, or they her, for anything less than an emergency (incidentally, the initial reason for getting them often starts with the former, then inevitably gives way to the latter). Of course, it goes without saying that being monitored this way will not always be appreciated by most kids, especially teenagers. It's not hard to imagine kids leaving their phones at a friend's house while they sneak someplace else, or more probably using Google, Siri, or TikTok to learn how to temporarily disable or disrupt the tracking settings. In any case, childhood, whether or not you had a good one, is one of those things you really can't adequately appreciate until it's over—often long after it's over. It's not that you didn't or couldn't appreciate those days as they were happening, it's just that *that* appreciation, on whatever level you felt and understood it, was entirely different from the view you have as an adult, looking down, as it were, from a good deal higher up the mountain. Aided by the wisdom that age and experience typically confer, hindsight affords a unique and advantaged perspective from which to draw insights and conclusions, and among these I aim to explore here the role that a lack of supervision, most notably during childhood, plays in shaping our experiences, particularly who we become as a result and the broader implications of how we think about all this in hindsight.

Incidentally, wouldn't it be interesting to know how many of your childhood experiences, percentagewise, were unsupervised? Just think how many of the things you learned, for better or for worse, were initiated by the words "let's see what happens," which is essentially the scientific method and is usually employed much more liberally in the absence of supervision, especially adult supervision.

By the providential grace of God, I happen to be one of those fortunate souls who got to experience youth before the full-scale invasion of the Internet and cellular technology. There were certainly plenty of promising technological innovations to enjoy back then, especially in contrast to our parents' and grandparents' generations, but compared to everything we take for granted these days, even *my* spoiled generation was in the Stone Ages—though maybe that's what every generation thinks about the ones that came before theirs. However, as primitive as some of those technologies now seem—the Polaroid camera is one example—it's important to remember with sincere appreciation that each one played its own particular role as a steppingstone in the evolutionary pathway of technological progress that has led us to where we currently are, a time when the advent of each new breakthrough almost makes you want to cringe. Like the surveillance technology utilized by my friend, for example, or the latest such technology for the home, which you can now carry with you wherever you go, receiving real-time notifications on your smartphone the moment someone approaches your property, even if you are thousands of miles away. And while it's easy to imagine how useful such technologies must be in many ways to parents and non-parents alike, I couldn't be more thankful that they weren't around to spoil the footloose and fancy-free unsupervised gallivanting that defined so much of my own childhood.

Although my sister and I were blessed to have a mom who stayed home with us until we started school, she soon thereafter joined Dad in working full-time throughout our childhood, which meant that most days we kids had pretty free reign from the time we left school until they got home around five p.m. This made us unwitting members of a sociological category we would only discover years later in college, namely *latchkey children*—meaning kids who after school gained access to an empty house through a key left under the doormat, or in our case in the garage. And while some of the potential mischief we might have gotten into during those hours was mitigated by the innumerable hours we spent planted in front of the television, there was still plenty of time for us to pretty much do as we pleased, often roaming on our bikes as far as two or three miles across town without any supervision but the company of friends. Even when our parents were home or they left a babysitter to look after us, we still had plenty of liberty most of the time to go pretty much wherever we wanted. At most we might have left behind a note saying where we were headed, with whom, and when we might be back, though of course that was prone to change on a whim and therefore wasn't much better than no note at all. You might think it was unwise or irresponsible for our parents to allow us to wander so freely this way, but this wasn't because they didn't care. Far from it. Nor do I think it had much to do with the particular era of the mid-seventies and eighties, which, while much different culturally than now, was in many ways just as potentially hazardous. More probably the apparent looseness of their policy, which seemed to be a common one at the time, had more to do with their understandable assumption that in most cases things would probably be okay in little-old Huron, South Dakota. They also happened to be God-fearing Christians, which additionally undergirded that trust. At any rate, whatever a parent's trust level in this regard, at the end of the day there is only so much you can do to protect your kids, unsupervised or otherwise. And again, had the house been rigged inside and out with cameras connected to parental smartphones, and had we also been forced to carry tracking devices of our own everywhere we went, I hate to think how dull those adventuresome days would have been, almost like being on house arrest.

Of course, all this unsupervised independence I enjoyed so much at the time—and even now also, as an adult, appreciate having had—I appreciate as one who has no children of his own. That is to say this status obviously makes it easier to feel this way, since doing so doesn't result in the cognitive dissonance I would likely have to endure if I did have my own kids and chose to apply a drastically different policy in their case, namely a much more stringent one. And this in spite of the fact that I am also one who has a firm trust in God. Which is to say I truly have to hand it to parents who are able to let their kids roam freely out of sight for extended periods like this, even if not to the extent that my sister I and some of our friends relished. Presuming you truly love them, it really is a significant act of faith to let go of your kids this way, even temporarily, even while using the tracking apps, especially before they reach the semi-self-sufficiency of their teens. Though I suppose it's no different then either, since, regardless of how independent they are, anything can happen at any time, and they are irreplaceable (at least in the sense that each is one-of-a-kind and infinitely precious). And while bad things can happen in the presence of supervision just as much as they can in its absence, we are prone to think—both with and without sufficient justification—that it's more likely in the latter case.

At any rate, it's only as a childless bachelor reflecting on my childhood this way that in theory I object to the use of resources like the tracking apps, since they really aren't much different than having your kids on a leash. But force me to imagine for a moment having hypothetical children of my own, and my reasoning suddenly turns on a dime. Only then does the idea seem reasonable, along with a robust household surveillance system, and possibly more, if there is more, short of actual shackles or shock collars. That is, if you expect me to survive parenthood without suffering, at the minimum, a heart attack a week (hey, if my hypothetical kids have to pay the price for my insecurity, so be it). Though on the other hand, envisioning myself regularly monitoring the whereabouts and doings of my temporarily unsupervised imaginary children seems like it might be stressful enough in itself, maybe even worse than the alternative.

Besides this irony related to me personally, another is just as interesting to highlight, namely that, as necessary as supervision and boundaries are to our development as children into healthy, well-balanced adults, kids also need to experience life without supervision. The word *need* here is meant to suggest that being raised under constant supervision would result in something less than a mentally and socially well-adjusted adult. Whether in the company of companions or by ourselves, it is when we are unsupervised that we are truly tested as to how we will make independent decisions for ourselves, for better and for worse. It measures the mettle of our character in a different way than when we are being monitored, even somewhat loosely. Situations where we don't have mommy or daddy or teachers there to protect us or answer our questions, when we have to decide on the spot whether we will go along with the crowd or stand our ground in defense of principle or the minority position. We need room to be able to choose for ourselves between right and wrong, good and evil, apart from the constraints imposed by adults. Moreover, we all know the critical importance of being allowed to make mistakes as part of the learning process, even when it means failing miserably. In fact, failing is often just as important as getting it right—to be sure, in many cases the former necessarily precedes the latter.

Just imagine if we lived our entire childhood, not to mention our whole lives, under the taut umbrella of nonstop supervision, how drastically different the world would be. On the one hand, presumably there would be substantially less outward disobedience—less lying, less theft, less adultery, less murder. Which sounds pretty good until you ask: What good is obedience born of compulsion? Don't we call that *subservience* or *fealty*, both of which have negative connotations? Whether this scenario seems better or worse than a life without any supervision whatsoever, both options differ drastically from that which most of us have had the high privilege of taking for granted, which allows one a reasonably measured combination of the two. And in either case we generally have the liberty in most circumstances to freely choose between right and wrong in accord with the light of conscience and whatever ethics we have been taught. In contrast, picture images you have seen of broad streams of North Korean or Chinese soldiers marching lockstep in flawless cadence before the gleeful cheering of servile crowds, plenty of whom surely do not feel inwardly what they are expressing outwardly. How can they do otherwise with Big Brother breathing down their neck twenty-four-seven? On the other hand, lack of supervision generally results in an increase of rule and law breaking, no matter a person's age, both privately and publicly, so clearly a balance is needed. At any rate, just imagine how much different you would be—your essential character—how differently you would think and act, if your every experience were supervised, whether just during childhood or from the cradle to the grave. In either case the lion's share of your behavior might be little more than a façade, a pretense to avoid the consequences of noncompliance.

But before exploring more deeply another angle in connection with these ideas, as well as their implications, it may be helpful to illustrate the above with more specific practical examples of what such freedom entails, which will also serve as a reference point for the second half of the essay. And in keeping with the personal nature of this piece, please indulge me to offer as examples a handful of particularly memorable unsupervised adventures from my own childhood that were the first among many to volunteer themselves.

The first of these is probably the most poignant. Picture a grubby pair of twelve-year-old boys leaving an empty house just south of town one morning or afternoon to go on what had become routine little "exploring" expeditions whenever the two got together, which usually involved venturing a few blocks away at the most, as far as a nearby pond where the two discovered the usual boyhood thrills of frogs and toads to skip like stones across the water, or cattails to crush in their hands. And because on this occasion neither of my buddy's parents were home, we needed no permission and thus decided to wander several blocks beyond the pond to Highway 37, which we apparently crossed beneath the bridge there, sliding in our tennis shoes across the slippery surface of the narrow creek called Stony Run, fascinated by the frogs frozen just beneath. Emerging on the other side, we marched aimlessly eastward, where the creek broadens slightly into the misnomer that is Stony Run Lake for about three quarters of a mile until it narrows again before meeting the James River. Looking at a map now, it appears that at our farthest point away we may have walked anywhere from a mile to two miles from his house. I don't remember the month, but there were at least a couple inches of snow on the ground, and I think at one point we came within about a hundred feet from what I remember to be a dilapidated wooden bridge to nowhere, though Google Maps reveals nothing of the sort. Nevertheless, it was there that the ice seemed to be frozen into multiple smooth humps a few feet high each, which hindsight tells me were probably snow-covered muskrat or beaver lodges, which I fleetingly recall us sliding down on our butts, until the next thing I knew my friend was flailing his arms in the open water a few feet from me, and a few moments later I was somehow—sometimes I think with angelic assistance—pulling him out without falling through myself, though I have no recollection of this. Then, without either of us saying anything either of us can remember, we simultaneously turned to trek the long way back, my dear friend shivering terribly with teeth literally chattering as we trudged arm-in-arm through the blowing snow, eventually, finally, after what must have taken at least half an hour, reaching his house, where we quickly stripped to our underwear and thawed our scrawny little bones by the sweet-smelling warmth of a kerosene heater.

I've had some close calls over the years, but this one holds a special place for me. Not only was my friend's life spared, so was mine, and both in what I consider a miraculous way. Sometimes I shudder to think how irreparably devastated our families would have been if we had both disappeared beneath the ice out there in the middle of nowhere without anyone knowing where we were. The thought of their immeasurable pain in having lost us is one thing, but substantially more unfathomable is the thought of the prolonged torture of their frantic searching in vain, perhaps even for years thereafter, baffled as to how we could have simply vanished into thin air. Or similarly, the thought of how traumatized my own life might have been—in addition to everyone else's grief—if I hadn't been able to fish out my dear friend and had to live with that guilt and regret the rest of my life. And yet I still treasure the memory, especially the fact that we were allowed the opportunity of the unsupervised experience that made it possible—if for no other reason than to be able to share it like this, trusting that, like so many other such stories, the effect it may leave on the thinking of some readers will by itself make it worth the experience.

I remember so many adventures involving the notorious McNutt brothers, who moved in across the street when I was six or seven years old. The younger of the two, nicknamed "Icky" (or "Ick" for short), though a couple years older than I was, quickly became one of my most constant companions for the next several years. With him and his older brother I spent countless unsupervised hours—in fact, almost exclusively unsupervised hours—during which I was continually learning all sorts of new and fascinating skills. Like how to swear, first of all, which is to say prodigiously; how to spit with attitude and force; to play Spin the Bottle and Truth or Dare; to catch nightcrawlers with my bare hands and a flashlight in the backyard lawn on a rainy night, even during a thunderstorm; to scale and gut crappies, bluegills, and perch; to cleverly overcome a locked patio door by lifting it just enough for the latch hook to slip over the jam plate (with which talent I shocked and impressed my older cousin Greg sometime thereafter when we came upon his brother's house one winter afternoon and I thereby gained us entrance). As part of our many fishing expeditions, we would ride our bikes with poles and bait and net and five-gallon bucket in hand down to the James River, about a mile away at our usual spot, just below what was then the undeveloped north end of Riverview Drive, down a fairly steep dirt trail surrounded by a dense cluster of trees, which eventually opened to a small clearing maybe fifteen feet square at the most, right at the water's edge, where the current flowed deceivingly gently over a shallow dam of rocks that I was often tempted to hop across to the other side, as I remember watching the eldest McNutt brother do at least once, and when he couldn't have been older than twelve or thirteen. As often as I think of this secluded spot—of which I'm pretty sure none of our parents were aware—I sometimes shudder to think how close the three of us stood to the water, sometimes on top of large or small rocks, and how ignorant we were of the river's powerful undertow. I cringe especially when I picture the many times we fished from the rock-lined platform another mile upstream, beside the Third Street dam, where I remember the river spilling gently over it into the frothing undertow. While in town for a recent visit, however, this same time-worn platform appeared exceedingly vulnerable beside what was a much more aggressive turbulence that looked like it could overtake the platform at any moment—the same dam that as a teenager I learned had once swallowed up a handful of shortsighted, unsupervised young men who tried canoeing over the deceptively short drop, which spot I have so many times recalled with a shiver at the morbid thought of one of us shoving the other off the platform as a joke, and what that would have meant.

Finally, from my first days of high school, that precious twilight phase separating childhood from young adulthood, how could I forget those crisp autumn evenings after dark during homecoming week, hopping in with a carload of buddies and a case of the cheapest toilet paper available, to make the rounds "tee-pee-ing" the trees at the houses of as many friends and sometimes teachers as our supply would allow? The hysterical laughter alone involved in this odd novelty the first time you did it was enough reward in itself for repeating the procedure in subsequent years and ensuring for it a lasting place in your memory (how did it possibly take us so long to discover such a blissful pastime?). This involved the dual challenge of tossing each roll just high and hard enough to reach the top center of a tree without overshooting it altogether, while at the same time releasing it with the quarterback-touch necessary to cause it to begin to unravel on the way up, so that its unpredictable branch-by-branch descent resulted in maximum distribution of the product—which is to say money well spent—which process was, of course, repeated until each tree was sufficiently woven through with this festive tinsel. But these coordinated strikes were not complete until the windows and rearview mirrors of any vehicles left outside were scribbled over with enough bar soap to cover them like frost, or with various messages, which might also be scrawled on the driveway or sidewalk or street—whether nicknames, inside jokes, or even just pride in one's own graduating class—*'93 Rulz*—thus partly betraying our identity. It really was quite the unique art project, the ultimate success of which could only be properly assessed in the light of the following morning's sunrise as you slowly drove through town proudly admiring the haunting spectacle of your handiwork.

The point of these examples isn't so much the details—though they are also relevant—but to draw attention to the common thread weaving them (and so many others like them) together, which not only made them possible but allowed them to take the particular shape they did, which consequently shaped my comrades and me in the particular way they did. Had there been the least adult supervision within a stone's throw of any of these activities, most of them probably wouldn't have happened, or at least not the same way—which is to say that in all likelihood they wouldn't have been nearly as enjoyable, nor as memorable, nor as able now, so many years later, to make me smile and laugh and cringe and shake my head.

ৎৎ৽৽

But just beneath the surface of this last idea there's a surprising objection lurking that takes this conversation to another level: *So what* if certain unsupervised experiences were enjoyable at the time, and *so what* if the memory of them now makes you smile and laugh and appreciate having had them?

I alluded earlier to the apparent downside, the negative connotation, sometimes associated with a lack of supervision, namely that it generally makes mischief more likely. And while the absence of authoritative oversight certainly plays an important role in whether or not we misbehave, it is not the *central* reason we do. Whether we are children (including teenagers) or adults, whether or not we are supervised, our real problem lies in our nature—our inborn disposition and default setting—which, despite its well-meaning pretensions to the contrary, chafes at the notion of being restrained. At being told we are not allowed to do something or other, or that we should do it in some way other than the way *we* want to do it. This is our innate propensity from the time we are toddlers, to want this sort of autonomy all the time. The fact that we label the stage during which the first signs of this proclivity become undeniable as *The Terrible Twos* should tell us *something*, shouldn't it? Moreover, this intrinsic brokenness is the ultimate source of all human strife and dissolution, what makes friendship and marriage and the cohesiveness of societies in general so challenging, and so respectable and impressive when they prosper and endure. And of course this has everything to do with morality, the Tree of the Knowledge of Good and Evil. So far it has only been suggested that *some* lack of supervision during childhood is necessary for the healthy, balanced formation of our personality and character, and that many such experiences would almost certainly have been less fun and interesting—not to mention safer and differently formative—if they had been supervised. At no point, however, including now, has this been to imply that the less supervision we have in our youth (let alone in adulthood), the better. That is an entirely different proposition. But circling back to the opening objection that started us in this new direction, the idea is to take a step beyond the initial observation of how a lack of supervision makes a critical difference in determining the nature of our experiences, and consequently the content of our character, to considering some further practical implications of this, which are of no small import. And some of these implications will be revealed by boiling down this new approach to the conversation to this question: Is it possible—without compromising your moral and logical integrity—to appreciate certain former unsupervised experiences which you now consider morally wrong?

But before we scamper down this rabbit hole, is it even reasonable to assume that everyone reading this has a shared notion of what is meant by the phrase *morally wrong*? On the one hand, a person could argue that, in the strictest sense, all of our experiences, even our most commendable, are tainted with imperfection, however slight, and therefore fall short of a hypothetically impeccable, universally applicable, objective moral standard. Of course, it also goes without saying that someone else will strongly disagree with such an assessment. But for our purpose here, while the intended scope of this phrase (morally wrong) is fairly open-ended and may include offenses that some consider trivial in comparison to others, it does in fact assume that the vast majority of us—with the possible exception of the psychopath, sociopath, or the otherwise mentally impaired—share a common understanding of what it means to transgress, including how it feels, which is to say that we realize when we have done so (and more times than we can count, by the way), which means nearly everyone qualifies to face our central question and its implications.

It will be helpful to begin by saying a little more about how the concluding focus of the first half of the essay relates to the provocative question just proposed as our focus. On the one hand, we cannot deny that among the plethora of unsupervised experiences that have been instrumental in shaping us into the person we presently are, both for better and for worse, are included some which we consider morally wrong—and the argument being proposed thus far assumes that, despite our potentially numerous shortcomings of character, some of which are the direct or indirect result of such experiences, we are generally okay with the person staring back at us in the mirror, which means that we must in some sense approve of the role these played in shaping us so. Without these experiences, without those choices we made, however wrong any of them may have been, we wouldn't be the same person we are today. Like it or not, even the lack of just one of them would make us either slightly or substantially different from who we actually are. Whether or not we now regret any, many, or all such decisions and experiences, the fact is each played its own particular role in molding our personality and character, and the aim here is to show that it's possible for us to appreciate the influence such experiences had on us, even negatively, without necessarily making us hypocrites or moral monsters or blasphemers for thinking so—that is, so long as one recognizes that one, and only one, worldview makes this possible, the rudimentary contours of which will be explored shortly. From the handful of fistfights I got into on the walk to and from Madison School to the unmentionable things, both legal and illegal, that I, with and without my buddies, got into during our teens, some of the things I learned thereby, for better and for worse, were in many cases the result of going places and doing things I shouldn't have, violating taboos and conscience and the positive values instilled in me at home and school and church. Whether such choices and actions were motivated by fear, perceived necessity, or simply the desire to please myself or my peers, they played their role in helping to lay the foundation of my personality, on which the remaining scaffolding of my adult character would eventually be built.

Viewed from this angle, in this light, this negative aspect, so to speak, of our unleashed history is not necessarily an altogether bad thing. In fact to some degree, absent divine intervention, given our natural inclination to carry out nearly every whim that issues from our wayward hearts—especially considering the immaturity of mindset and disposition from which all these experiences sprang—so much of it seems practically inevitable. Incidentally, why we don't give way to *every* errant impulse is another fascinating angle equally worthy of more attention than simple mention, though for our purpose here it is more than we need to pursue. Though it goes without saying that at the time you were not thinking about how a given choice or act might shape you or anyone else from that point forward, it's nevertheless critical to recognize that we are accountable for having made those choices and done those things, as far as their repercussions for us or for others, both at the time and to this day and beyond. Yet just because many of these experiences may be regrettable doesn't necessarily mean they were wasted or pointless. While it may be true that making better choices at such times might have shaped us or others in a morally superior way, what if certain less-than-noble choices or actions turned out to yield positive, even beneficial, results somewhere down the causal chain? What if certain ends, however few or many, might have been more effectually brought to pass thereby than through some other more acceptable means, morally speaking? What if all of these regrettable choices and experiences do not just happen randomly or without purpose, but rather play essential roles in the broader scheme of things? All of which questions should give us pause to ask yet another: What if our typical, superficial ways of thinking about and accounting for such things are woefully shortsighted and inadequate? Basic preliminary questions like these ought to caution the skeptic from clinging too tenaciously to the notion that no good could possibly come from such choices and behaviors, which we could even label as sinful or evil. In fact, as we will see, the implications of believing this are more dire than a person might initially be tempted to expect.

Of course, on their face, such audacious claims as we are proposing do cry out to be justified, though obviously attempting to climb such a steep and slippery slope calls for as much humility as caution.

This brings us back to the objection proposed earlier, which rightly wonders whether a person can simultaneously disapprove of and yet also appreciate (i.e. approve of) the same experience. At surface level, we may hear or read this and think nothing of it, as far as why it might be problematic. But you may have noticed in this last restatement that a key portion—in fact, *the* key portion—of the initial question is missing, namely: *without compromising your moral and logical integrity*. This phrase reveals that the intention of the question is not concerned merely with a person's volitional *ability* to simultaneously approve and disapprove of the same decision or act—which obviously anyone can do—but rather to highlight the implications of doing so. This is to say there are *two* aspects of our credibility at stake here, and undermining either necessarily means our position is either logically or morally untenable, or both—none of which we want to be the case if we hope to win the respect of others, not to mention our own.

Let's start with the *rational* part of our integrity. Isn't it fallacious logic, a clear violation of the law of non-contradiction, to say that we appreciate (i.e. approve of) something of which we ultimately disapprove? At first, these conflicting ideas do seem to be mutually exclusive, and therefore logically problematic. But are they really? Conservative political commentator Ben Shapiro, a careful thinker and communicator, often reiterates the helpful, reliable axiom: "Two things can be true at once." When he says this, he means that, just because two or more ideas may seem to stand in stark contrast to one another, this tension doesn't automatically, formally invalidate them, nor our ability to believe them simultaneously. But if this axiom is to apply to our present statement and it isn't in fact contradictory, what, we should ask, would have to be true about it (the statement, not the axiom)? Answer: that it assumes that the approving and disapproving are not being done in precisely the same sense. That is, if the disapproval in view is wholehearted and absolute—which it is—and the appreciation, or approval, is only to some degree, or partial—which it is—the two ideas are not really mutually exclusive, therefore the law of non-contradiction is not compromised, and consequently no longer threatens to render both our question and reasoning as nonsensical.

But even if this validation of our rational approach allows us temporary refuge from the crosshairs of this aspect of the objection, we still need to justify ourselves on moral grounds. If, as mentioned earlier, we concede that wrong is wrong, regardless of degree, how can we still stand by our argument? In other words, even if we only in some sense approve of (i.e. appreciate) that of which we also wholeheartedly disapprove, we are still approving of something we consider to be wrong, which would seem to make us morally compromised. In fact, we may rightly wonder whether our supposed "wholehearted" disapproval is truly that if to any degree we approve of that thing. So how can we reconcile these in a manner that preserves our moral integrity? As mentioned earlier, many unsupervised experiences spawned from the naivety of my often-unbridled childhood still make me laugh as I remember them—but what of their sometimes negative, harmful elements? Should any fond or lighthearted remembrance or appreciation I may have of them be tolerated, or should this rather be construed as the death knell of whatever degree of moral integrity I claim to hold?

Whatever else it means to embrace the apparent inconsistency of looking at things from this standpoint, at the very least it means that just because you no longer believe certain choices or behaviors from your unsupervised childhood are right and don't wish to repeat them doesn't necessarily mean you wish you never experienced such, though in many, or even most, cases you might feel this way, and strongly so, and rightly. In favor of this partial appreciation and approval aspect—two things can be true at once—you recognize that some of these experiences taught you invaluable lessons, some of which you may not even yet be conscious, and which you might not have been able to learn any other way, even when—in some cases especially when—disaster was breathtakingly close, whether or not you realized it. Even as a prepubescent, if I hadn't disobeyed, I wouldn't have been spanked, and if I hadn't been spanked I wouldn't be the same person I presently am. That is, through disobedience I gained something positive, even beneficial—there's a paradox for you—namely the lessons I learned through those whippings, which stick with me to this day, whether I realize it or not—and I learned plenty, believe me, at the very least how to avoid the next one (at least in theory). But this sounds an awful lot like trying to justify bad behavior, and how can we claim to do that without simultaneously compromising our moral probity? See where this is going? And this is important to point out since this whole matter is one of principle. Just as the law of non-contradiction compels us to nullify two mutually exclusive ideas, so approving of wrongdoing, regardless of degree, renders us immoral at that point, at least in the strictest sense.

On the one hand, I treasure the fact that I was allowed sufficient liberty to explore and discover exhilarating as well as painful and sometimes dangerous and regrettable experiences without being sheltered or tracked everywhere I went—even when that meant the chance to try things like taking a turn too fast with friends and no seatbelts on a remote gravel road, the old brown Buick skidding sideways-backwards into a ditch and through some farmer's barbed-wire fence, the fear and adrenaline burning through me like fire, or the chance to feel the sharp, unmistakable sting of guilt after having shoplifted for the first time (a single pack of grape bubblegum). Had adequate supervision prevented me from experiencing such situations and others, some through which I had to persevere, gritting my teeth, I very well may not be in possession of the tender conscience or stubborn resilience or some other quality I take for granted—each of which, despite their drawbacks, have nevertheless served me well in various ways through the years. After all, it's not just prescriptive moral codes that teach us right from wrong, but often guilt and regret— and not just after the transgression but sometimes even leading up to and while you're in the very act, when you know what you're doing is wrong but you do it anyway. Reflecting on these things thereafter, whether moments or years later, persistent conviction often compels you to do better next time, to learn from your mistakes and transgressions, regardless of whether you choose to comply. It's one thing to be guided by rules or principles you've been taught, but quite another to be admonished by the inescapable, unmistakable, invaluable, inborn voice of self-denunciation that Adam Smith called "the impartial spectator"—which guidance precepts alone cannot in the same way impart. It's this guidance that tells you what to do about the precepts in terms of "should," what philosopher Immanuel Kant referred to as the "categorical imperative."

For the most part it's impossible for us to know what exactly it is about a given experience that winds up fashioning our character so uniquely, thereby making us the one-of-a-kind irreplaceables we are—and again, to keep this discussion simpler and more concise, the scope here has been restricted only to our unsupervised childhood experiences, though obviously our supervised ones shape us in their own peculiar ways (I'm also thinking mainly of those experiences that involved choices *we* made, rather than those in which the choices of others affected us, though ultimately both are in view). This is to say, in a way that brings to mind Jesus' parable of the wheat and the weeds[1] (though only as a partial metaphor), that getting rid of the latter—if we had the option of doing so—might mean destroying the former in the process. By this I mean that the "field" of who we are is in part composed of our collective good and bad unsupervised experiences, and though we may wish to forget or distance ourselves from any or many of these formative events, without them, even the "weeds"—both the experiences themselves and what remains of our memories of them—we wouldn't be quite the same personality we take for granted.[2]

But this brings us to the other hand, and right back to the same conscientious objector, who still isn't satisfied with such logic. *So what*, he says, if such experiences in that unfettered past of yours played some role in shaping you into the person you currently are? Are you trying to say that just because the collective whole of those experiences, or even just the ones of which you now disapprove, wound up influencing your persona in a way that you, or others, find acceptable, that you can so easily sidestep the charge of moral inconsistency? Suppose we up the ante by getting more specific, and ask: What if more serious atrocities like arson, rape, or murder were among those adventures? Dare you still insist that even such crimes are justifiable (to be appreciated) simply because without having done them you wouldn't be quite who you are?

You see now just how treacherous this path is that we are carefully attempting to climb. A person is sometimes tempted to think he can think whatever and however he wants, though obviously your approach will determine the content of your character—though your character, likewise, determines your approach—and consequently your reputation. And what sane person wants to have his manner of reasoning compared with the likes of Ted Bundy or Tim McVeigh? That is to say, on the one hand, we dare not ignore the implications of this last objection, and yet neither dare we concede this to be the final word on the subject.

While it can't be denied that every unsupervised choice we've made and course we've taken has had some effect on our personality, for better or for worse, in order to offer a winning answer to this last objection we must go further than simply restating this fact. Back in the first half of this essay, we noticed that perspective makes all the difference as to whether or not, and to what extent, we appreciate the role of supervision—depending in some cases on whether the question is being considered by a child or an adult, or in any case on whether the supervision proves a hindrance to getting what we want. In a similar way, our perspective is what really makes the difference as to how we view our general moral standing before God and man, which is what we're concerned about here in trying to offer a persuasive answer to how we can on any level, for any reason, appreciate sub-moral choices or experiences without compromising our ethics.

But the first thing to recognize as we reflect on such, or any, of our misdeeds, past or present, is that there is in our fallen

158 | Ted Stamp

nature an insidious, diabolical tendency to dismiss or diminish any guilt we may feel on account of having done them, including whatever negative effects they have wrought in our personality or that of others, and to what extent we are ultimately accountable for them (the deeds themselves as well as their effects). This perspective of self-justification and self-preservation, a kind of survival instinct, often seems reasonable to us because, in contrast to the previous idea, we recognize that some of the effects of these unsupervised decisions have been positive, like shaping our personality in some ways for good (though, of course, it goes without saying that whether we or others are the judge of what is and is not "good" in this respect, such judgment is merely subjective, which is to say biased and fallible). Not only that, who we were back when we did these things is far removed from who we are now, so this, too, can lead us to think it's not such a big deal if we simultaneously appreciate and disapprove of some of these experiences. Sometimes we are even tempted to think that, had we been then who we are now, we would not have made such choices. But not only can we not know whether or not that is true, the ironic fallacy of thinking this way is that we wouldn't be who we are now without having made those choices—not to mention all the rest between then and now—which is to say we might not think this if on one or more of those occasions we had chosen differently. Besides, most of the time we take completely for granted who we are and what exactly has made us this way, and for the most part those experiences don't seem to us nearly as bad when we compare them to those of others, especially to extreme examples like those raised by the objector a moment ago, as if rating them on a moral spectrum makes a difference—regardless of where each of these choices and behaviors rate on the scale, the fact is each one, no matter how petty, falls short of Good. Nevertheless, like it or not, it's often easier for us to see the problem with justifying bad choices and behavior when we are confronted by the extremes, especially when they are hypothetical, or not our own—when it's *our* conduct under scrutiny, we tend to find ways to justify the extremes as much as all lesser offenses.

In stark contrast to the above perspective, the worldview for which we have been gradually working toward making a sensible case in no way seeks to downplay or avoid the acceptance of guilt or accountability for any past wrongs of which we or anyone else are culpable. On the contrary, in keeping with the notion mentioned earlier that, in the strictest sense, wrong is wrong regardless of degree, this liberating perspective welcomes the honesty, humility, and transparency that necessarily precedes the willingness to confess and forsake every choice and experience for which we feel the least regret or shame. Far from fearing the prospect of the eventual administration of perfect Justice one day at the impeccably competent discretion of the one and only transcendent Source and embodiment of everything True and Good, this perspective embraces and celebrates the fact. This argument even goes so far as to suggest that this is the *only* perspective, or worldview, that truly allows a person to be justified in appreciating in some limited sense the kind of experiences we've been discussing without approving of their sub-moral aspects—in fact, while strongly denouncing any and all of these.

Still, this daring claim that such experiences may "play essential roles in the broader scheme of things," potentially even yielding "positive, even beneficial results," doesn't yet satisfy the conscientious objector, since these ideas may be construed to reduce or nullify the wrongness of the choices and acts that in some way led to these results. In other words, if the implication of the claim we are making is that the overall End—as well as all lesser, intermediate ends—brought about in such cases are said to justify the means used to bring them about, it shouldn't surprise us that the same objection is raised as the one that initiated this half of the essay, since they are essentially the same, based on the very same principle: *So what* if the effects of certain unsupervised choices and behaviors have served practical or utilitarian ends (like, as we have already said, shaping our character in positive ways, or creating memories we appreciate in some sense and to some degree)? If in the process of any of these transactions objective moral values or principles have been violated—which in the strictest sense they have—how can this be overlooked?

But before exploring the remaining and central features of this worldview being proposed to effectively answer questions like the above, attention should be drawn to what is implied by such persistent objections, namely their concern for such a breach of propriety, because the answer to them is at the heart of this entire conversation and is actually the basis for its legitimacy. And what their concern implies is what we have been assuming all along without needing to state explicitly: that human beings, in their general approach to nearly all practical matters—as opposed to what they may think hypothetically or philosophically—take for granted that morality is not relative. That is, we live our lives under the implicit assumption that our everyday engagement with the world and one another is not an illusion, but rather is both guided and undergirded by a basic set of universal moral precepts that we did not choose or create—what the famed apologist C. S. Lewis referred to as the "Law of Human Nature, or Moral Law, or Rule of Decent Behaviour"[3]—a system governed by a sense of ought, at any rate something more than mere personal preference, since it goes without saying that a worldview characterized chiefly by an insipid platitude like "you have your truth and I have mine" is the hallmark of the ignoramus and the very starting point for the loss of all true meaning and purpose, and consequently the breakdown of civil society in general. Without an objective moral framework to ground everything one thinks and does, morality becomes relative, which is to say all things become permissible, meaning that one no longer needs to justify to himself or anyone else sufficient reason for pursuing a given course—which policy is, of course, thoroughly arbitrary and ad hoc, whatever seems expedient to suit one's constantly fluctuating inclinations at any given moment. In other words, survival of the fittest, or *Might makes right*, in which case metaphysical concepts like "right" and "wrong" are meaningless, since they mean different things to each person. And if this cardinal presupposition is granted—that this Law of Human Nature is the necessary prerequisite for a conversation like this (not to mention all others) to have real meaning—this necessarily implies the existence of a metaphysical "Something which is directing the universe, and which appears in me as a law urging me to do right and making me feel responsible and uncomfortable when I do wrong"[4] (C. S. Lewis), an eternal, unchanging, intelligent, personal Giver, or Source, of those objective moral absolutes—what Anselm of Canterbury referred to as "that than which nothing greater can be thought"—since we should hardly be expected to believe that even the crudest of ethical principles can come from that which is inherently impersonal, unintelligent, and non-purposeful in its constitution, character, and conduct (e.g. Darwinistic materialism).

Now, in order to help account for what may appear to be the moral inconsistency of this worldview we have spilled so much ink attempting to describe and defend thus far, we need to bring into the conversation an aspect that has been hashed over for millennia by philosophers, theologians, and other curious folks. The formal labels most often attached to this conversation, usually in more academic settings, are The Problem of Evil, or Theodicy, the heart of which discussion is essentially concerned with providing a plausible and just explanation for how an allegedly all-powerful, all-knowing, perfectly-wise, perfectly-just, perfectly-loving and righteous Deity/Creator can truly be the possessor of such attributes while simultaneously permitting seemingly limitless evil to persist within the world He initially (allegedly) created to be without it. What exactly this apologetic looks like differs slightly from thinker to thinker, and over the centuries countless articles, books, and seminars have been devoted to the subject, expositing and defending it much more thoroughly and skillfully than this present effort will attempt. The aim here is merely to offer a concise summary of this approach as being adequate to resolve the central objections on the table, especially focusing on why and how this framework enables a person to maintain his moral and logical credibility while approving of that which he disapproves in the manner we have been outlining.

Before saying any more about this approach, though, it may be helpful first to hear how the skeptical objector often mounts his assault upon it:

Say we grant your premise that all things that exist were made by some Almighty Being with attributes as you have claimed. Doesn't perfect wisdom and omniscience presuppose the foresight to predict what grievous harm could come if the beings of "His" own "good" design became unhinged from their initial, unblemished state? Then why allow it to happen at all, much less permit it to reign unchecked thereafter (even mortal man, for all his faults, can see no sense in this)? Unless these "perfect" attributes—including the authority and power to intervene—are not so perfect after all? No wonder then that evil holds perpetual dominion over good. No wonder these alleged attributes are not as awe-inspiring as the most naïve and gullible seem to think. No wonder multitudes for ages have thought as multitudes still do: if "He" exists at all, it's only as a figment of the mind.

You see, beneath the well-composed veneer of the natural mind and heart, there lies a dark suspicion that there's something fraudulent about the claim that every absolute derives from a single, self-sufficient Source. In fact, in fairness, the claim that such an Entity exists by sheer necessity, uncaused, is not exactly easy for even the strongest of believers to embrace (that's partly why they call it faith). That every effect must have a cause—what philosophy calls the Law of Causality—is as fundamental to the way we think and live as the laws we covered earlier. Which means this concept of the underived explodes the circuits of the finite mind. To ask for the cause behind *this kind* of Cause is to miss the meaning of *underived*. Since this kind of Cause is *not* an effect, but rather the only true and necessary, uncaused given, the Law of Causality doesn't apply—how could it when, like every other law, it's just another product of this first and foremost self-existent Cause? Thus, the restless backward search for another such Cause is, by necessity, an infinite exercise in futility, since it can never arrive at an ultimate Cause—in fact, much less, it can only discover an eternal regress of immeasurably inferior finite causes. No wonder Aristotle settled for an anonymous *Unmoved Mover* behind everything that is. And yet no wonder, too, that so many others in the searching process only find frustration, indignation, alienation, disillusionment.

On the one hand, this impassioned search within man's weary heart for something bigger and deeper than himself is actually rooted in how he's been designed—that is, as some have put it, with *a God-shaped hole* at the center of his being, which also longs for wrong to be put right—another unmistakable hint and symptom, like the Law of Right and Wrong[5] within, that the Source from which he ultimately came is much higher and greater than Darwin's "warm little pond" (the ultimate source of which his famous theory can't explain). On the other hand, this seemingly noble desire in man is latent, at best. Born of the same infernal heart that drives his deepest doubts, this default guiding principle compels him to mistrust, resist, and, as often as possible, reject the supervisory rule of any other than his own. And never is this more true than when it comes to this most sovereign, ultimate Source, since doing so not only puts him in charge, it conveniently alleviates his conscience of its guilt—which is to say it leaves him free to do as he pleases without the fear of having to one day give account to some transcendent Judge.

So, while there's nothing wrong with asking probing questions as to why the created order happens to be the way it is, the finite creature, aware in his most unguarded moments of how little he actually understands, should beware of doing so irreverently—that is, in less than an honest pursuit of truth, as though to put God on trial. After all ...

What if—as far too few seem willing to concede, if only for the sake of argument—the ways and means of such a Being are beyond our present capacity to understand?

What if what seems to human beings like sheer indifference toward their sorrow and suffering, however insignificant or great, is light years from the actual truth?

What if, in fact, He's actually intervening more often than we know, preventing more sorrow and suffering than would otherwise come to pass without such help?

What if it just so happens such a Being has had a higher Purpose for allowing evil temporarily—that, like a dog on a leash, it's been allowed to play a critical, carefully restricted role within the confines of a greater Plan?

What if since the birth of time and space there's never been an action short of Good that hasn't been used by its Great Designer and Sustainer toward the outworking of a higher and greater End than was intended by those who with blissful indifference committed such?

What if, in spite of disapproving of the immoral nature of all such actions and their disastrous effects, this Being has found it fitting—in harmony with His flawless character—to patiently allow His creatures liberty to freely choose as they see fit within a given scope of constraints, all of which experiences He weaves together in such a way as to achieve His own superior Ultimate Good (including, in the process, innumerable lesser goods)?

Moreover—and this is the foundational cornerstone without which the framework cannot stand, and therefore loses its appeal—what if every choice and act of ours will one day receive its fitting recompense, whether for commendation or condemnation? This aspect of the framework means that when we say that we appreciate the fact that certain former experiences of which we now disapprove have played some part in shaping us into the person we presently are, we wish to point out that what may appear in some cases to be overlooking the bad because it has led to some good is not in fact what's going on. On the contrary, this *overlooking* would be more accurately described as trusting that every act of immorality, small or great, will ultimately be addressed—rather than ignored or overlooked—by a Judge of unimpeachable character on a scale we cannot now fully imagine or appreciate.

Of course, it goes without saying that the persuasive power and significance of this way of looking at things rests entirely on whether the Being we have briefly described actually exists. Nevertheless, that the nature, designs, and purposes of such may seem implausible or hard to comprehend does nothing to diminish their potential truthfulness.

So not only does this unparalleled framework offer an objective moral basis on which to ground a conversation like this, even as it promises the eventual administration of perfect justice for all, it maintains that even the worst human atrocities are being utilized in some way, big or small—whether sooner or later down the causal chain—to work toward the achievement of an ultimate Good, even if we can't discern the rhymes and reasons behind such intricate designs. Other beneficial reasons for embracing such a framework could also be detailed, but for our purpose here it will only be necessary to conclude with a few practical illustrations of what the above perspective looks like when actually applied to the human experience—specifically, how bad choices and behaviors can be the means for bringing about good, and Good, to which phenomenon countless men and women have for centuries borne witness, even to the present moment.

But first there is another crucial aspect of this discussion that hasn't yet been mentioned, namely what the permission of sin and suffering makes possible in a world like this. While a perfect world without either of these is what all human beings weary of this world's ways ultimately hope and long for, presumably such a world doesn't allow people to experience things like guilt and regret, which often lead to the willingness to offer an apology or to forgive, which sometimes lead to a substantial change for the better in the character and actions of those involved, and thereby also in the world in general. In a world or universe where nothing can go wrong, there is no need for apology, remedy, or repentance. There can be neither sickness nor sorrow, both of which, often to our surprise, can be great teachers and motivators. It takes a broken, less-than-perfect world like ours for any of these to have their place and play their role. From our admittedly foggy, finite point of view, we might be tempted to think that it would have been better if certain events and experiences didn't take place as they did, which is to say, in many cases, if we ourselves had made better choices—and in many cases that is very probably true. But the point is that we are obviously not in the position to say definitively one way or the other concerning any of these, since we lack the ability to trace the comprehensive chain reaction of results that follow any given choice or act to their ultimate conclusions (not only is the number of consequences that follow a given action, positive or negative, impossible for us to determine, we have no way to measure the extent or degree of their influence, such as whether or not a given "bad" action will ultimately wind up yielding more bad than good in the lives of all who are directly or indirectly touched by its effects). This is part of why it's not hard to believe that there are things which we could only learn by passing through certain less-than-optimal circumstances, which only a world like this makes possible, and at precise points in time and space with respect to the nature of our particular personality interacting with the equally unique personalities of others, shaping us at every point in very specific ways. Moreover, and central to our overall point here, none of this happens simply by chance. On the contrary, ensuring that we find ourselves at these particular times and places in order to be shaped in certain ways and for certain purposes is, among countless other things, the ultimate business of this Source we have in mind—though this shouldn't be construed to diminish the importance and significance of our ability to exercise our wills in any given situation, for better or for worse.

There is also a temptation to think that under no circumstances should we ever be thankful for sin and suffering and all the havoc they have wreaked, and that is certainly true to some degree. But by looking through the lens of this framework we have in mind—that is, from a Christian perspective—a person is challenged to broaden his outlook. This is because, on the one hand, while this Being with perfect attributes—especially righteousness, justice, and love—must necessarily hate the very concept and existence of sin and all it entails, on the other hand, without permitting its existence and pervasive influence in a world like this, certain redeeming features in it wouldn't be possible. Though a perfect world presumably has plenty of its own redeeming features, perhaps exponentially more than we can currently conceive, it seems reasonable to conclude that it cannot have the ones noted above and many others like them. Those who gladly embrace this way of understanding things recognize that, had it been better for this world to remain perfect, its perfectly capable Creator would not have allowed it to lapse into its present condition. And the fact that He did should at the very least give us pause to reflect on why that might be, though we need not resolve the tension and irony inherent in this paradox. It is enough just to stand back and accept in awestruck wonder.

Now, to demonstrate the practical interworking of the two sides of this reality—the enigmatic relationship between our own individual "free" will as creatures and the exhaustive, sovereign providence of the Creator over every last feature and experience throughout His creation—consider three examples that showcase all that we have attempted to make a plausible case for thus far. And since the specific identity of this framework is Christian, it is fitting that the clearest illustrations be supplied from the Judeo-Christian Scriptures. And for those who might be inclined to discount what follows simply on the basis that they don't believe the Christian Bible to be a credible source (let alone the only authoritative, trustworthy revelation of God's will for humanity), we could hope they might be so generous as to temporarily suspend such doubt until we've said all we have to say. And even if after hanging in there such skeptics are still not satisfied with what this worldview has to offer, it only seems fair to ask if they have a superior alternative to suggest.

We begin, fittingly, in the book of Genesis, not quite two thousand years before the birth of Christ, with the renowned story of Joseph,[6] the most beloved of the patriarch Jacob's twelve sons, whose jealous brothers sold him into slavery when he was just seventeen. This evil action, which brought him all the way from Canaan (i.e. Israel) to the house of Pharaoh, in Egypt, was soon followed by another when he found himself cast into prison after being falsely accused of sexual assault by the duplicitous wife of his new master. Yet in spite of all this injustice, in addition to the bitterness of having been separated from his father and family for about twenty years[7] as time wore on, Joseph was gradually granted sufficient favor to enable his ascending in rank to just below Pharaoh himself. Most of this authority was the reward for being the only one in Pharaoh's household able to provide a spot-on (God-given) interpretation for a perplexing dream Pharaoh had, which revealed that seven years of plenty were coming, followed by seven years of famine. So Joseph was appointed to oversee the storage of the bounty from the plentiful years, followed by the distribution thereof throughout the seven lean years. And lo and behold, before those lean years reached their end, multitudes from the surrounding regions began to arrive to beg for Pharaoh's help—most notable among them Joseph's brothers.

What transpires in the process is full of touching drama that culminates (spoiler alert) in Joseph tearfully divulging his true identity to his brothers, who are naturally shocked and fully expect him to take revenge for their betrayal. So when their father Jacob dies shortly after arriving and they begin to make a not-so-subtle appeal for mercy, they are amazed to hear their long-estranged brother respond: "As for you, you meant evil against me, but God meant it for good, to bring it about that many should be kept alive, as they are today."[8] He even explains that it was God himself, and not them, who sent him there.[9] Thus, in hindsight, both the victim and his victimizers were able to recognize and even appreciate how evil actions were not just permitted but utilized by God to achieve greater ends than any of them could have imagined or planned themselves (multitudes of which they didn't see, both during and after their lifetimes, at the very least in the lives of all who would read or hear of this account, including you and me). Moreover, the brothers explicitly acknowledging their own guilt in the matter clearly shows their own, and not God's, ultimate culpability for the wrong they did, for which they will one day face the consequences before Him. Meanwhile, for all who have eyes to see and ears to hear, the counterintuitive plans and ways of this inscrutable God are treasured by multitudes as glorious—including the fact that this historical miracle additionally serves as an uncanny pre-figure, or type, of an even greater, future betrayal of another Son by his own kindred.

This latter betrayal, of course, far and away the most egregious act of evil in all of history, was the crucifixion of the self-proclaimed Son of God, Jesus Christ, which served the ultimate purpose of opening the way for His sinful creatures to be reconciled to God—but again, not by means of a random series of historical accidents. On the one hand, unthinkable evil was permitted, which in one sense Christians could wish had not been allowed to happen. Yet without this terrible transaction there would be no hope for mankind beyond the grave—in fact, quite the opposite of hope. Again, Scripture, this time through the mouth of the apostle Peter fifty days after Jesus ascended to the right hand of His Father's throne in heaven, testifies to this mind-blowing mystery:

> Men of Israel, hear these words: Jesus of Nazareth, a man attested to you by God with mighty works and wonders and signs that God did through him in your midst, as you

yourselves know—this Jesus, delivered up according to the definite plan and foreknowledge of God, you crucified and killed by the hands of lawless men.[10]

That is, immeasurable evil perpetrated by human beings against the revealed will of their Creator—a will expressed through both external commandments like *Thou Shalt Not Kill*, and also through the internal witness of the conscience—for which they will be accountable to Him, was also somehow planned by Him in accord with an unrevealed aspect of His will to bring about something inexplicably good, yet without in the process violating either His faultless nature or the free agency of His creatures—for which He will be forever revered and magnified. Speaking along other, but similar lines to describe this mysterious method of the Almighty, thirteenth-century scholar Thomas Aquinas put it this way: "the operation of providence, whereby God works in things, does not exclude secondary causes, but, rather, is fulfilled by them."[11] No wonder the apostle Paul, in his celebrated letter to the church of God in Rome, climaxes his discussion of the big-picture Purposes of God with this befitting exultation:

> Oh, the depth of the riches and wisdom and knowledge of God! How unsearchable are his judgments and how inscrutable his ways! .... For from him and through him and to him are all things. To him be glory forever. Amen.[12]

Before considering one last example, consider a parable of Jesus[13] that will help further clarify this point. A moneylender had two debtors, the first of whom owed five hundred, and the other fifty. When neither could pay and both debts were canceled, Jesus asked which of them will love the moneylender more. The obvious answer was the one who was forgiven more, which is to say the one who owed the greater debt. The memorable line and central point with which Jesus drove home this lesson was: *the one who is forgiven little loves little.* In other words, the degree of one's appreciation for the degree to which he has been forgiven—especially in light of his inability to repay his debt—corresponds to the degree to which he will feel gratitude and love thereafter, and not only toward his debtor.

Finally, consider how the wrongdoing done by, and done to, the same individual on account of Jesus Christ resulted in, on the one hand, substantial suffering and sorrow, but on the other, immeasurable and everlasting good and joy. When we first encounter Saul of Tarsus in chapter nine of the Book of Acts (approximately five years after the death of Christ), religious zeal for the God of Judaism fuels his hate-breathing persecution of anyone associated with the allegedly resurrected "Messiah" from Nazareth.[14] This changes suddenly, however, when in a blinding blaze of glorious light this same resurrected rabbi breaks in on his furious pursuits, transforming him instantly (even his name, from Saul to Paul). So profound was this heavenly vision that he was compelled from that moment forward to endure for the risen Christ he had been persecuting steady seasons of hunger and thirst, shipwreck and robbery, severe and multiplied beatings, imprisonments, and eventually death by beheading. But it wasn't just that first unforgettable, supernatural encounter that God used to motivate His new apostle, but almost certainly also the memories of the many atrocities he had previously committed in ignorance.[15] In fact, it seems reasonable to conclude from his own testimony of such, in conjunction with the lesson of the parable just mentioned, that, had he not persecuted Christians to the extent that he did, in some cases to the death, the repentance that drove his tireless, redirected love and service for the Christ who had forgiven him for such might well have been less radical and risk-taking, which may have made him a less-effective ambassador for the faith than the one whose inspiring reputation is still famously remembered the world over. That is, he loved and served as much as he did at least partly because he recognized how much he had been loved and pardoned by the Master against whom he had so egregiously sinned. Moreover, both this remorse he felt and the intense persecution he suffered for the sake of this new endeavor shaped in very specific ways the content of his letters, which are a large part of his legacy, which for centuries have thereby blessed generations of Christians whose souls have been challenged and encouraged by them.

Once again, this last example shows how wrongdoing can ultimately play a pivotal role in leading to positive or commendable results. Yet none of these illustrations are meant either to encourage bad choices and behavior in order that good might result—a naïve and fatal error—or for that reason to dismiss the seriousness of even the least of these wrongs, even if some have in any way played some part in leading to some good, however small or great or seldom or often. Rather, these examples demonstrate that bad choices and behavior have long been and continue to be utilized by the all-sovereign Architect who is the very quintessence of Truth, Wisdom, and Good to bring about beneficial results in both the short and long term, whether anyone recognizes it or not. And the reason those who hold this worldview are justified in believing—with their logical and moral integrity intact—that it's possible to approve and disapprove of the same experience in different senses like this is *only* because they trust the testimony of such examples and others from Scripture, which reveal a larger Purpose for everything that happens under the sun (and beyond), good or bad, and that none of the latter is being overlooked. On the contrary, as we have already said, this Purpose includes the soon-approaching administration of perfect Justice

toward all of one's less-than-above-the-board decisions and behaviors, and because this is so, those who believe this can without
hesitation or equivocation speak the following truths in the same
breath: while sin is an abomination to be avoided at all costs, and
regretted and repented of as often as one knowingly or unknow-
ingly succumbs to its seductive allurements, that doesn't mean
that it and all the misery it has caused can't be salvaged, or har-
nessed, to some degree for Good, so long as the One in charge of
the process possesses the attributes and identity that have been
suggested.

But since those who espouse this worldview and those who
reject it are in the strictest sense equally guilty and deserving of
this perfect Justice at the discretion of their Creator, it's fair to ask
how this Justice will be applied in each case. And the first thing to
say about this is that the Justice of God doesn't come cheap. As we
have said, True Justice doesn't, and in fact can't, just sit idly by and
sweep wrongdoing under the rug, just as we would expect from
any earthly judge worth his salt. After all, if this One who is in
charge of all things truly possesses the attributes and identity we
have suggested, His perfect Justice *must* be satisfied—*propitiated*
is the biblical word—which is to say there must be penalties as-
signed for every transgression of that Justice, and His eternal nature determines the stakes. That is, the consequences in either
case necessarily extend interminably beyond this life, since, like
God, in whose image we were made, our souls and spirits are not
temporal. For those who gladly receive in exchange for their guilt
and shame the only available once-for-all-time sacrificial offering
(i.e. propitiation) of Jesus Christ on the cross on their behalf (the
righteous for the unrighteous), placing their trust in this perfect
(i.e. sinless) provision in order to receive forgiveness and recon-
ciliation from God, the result is unending joy and comfort,
whereas those who reject or neglect this free offer either wittingly

or unwittingly choose to bear this penalty themselves, the scope and severity of which they cannot now adequately appreciate (as for the chief characteristics of what this entails, consult the nearest New Testament).

On a more basic level, where this essay began, it's interesting to note the distinction between our supervised and unsupervised experiences and to appreciate the role of the latter in particular in shaping the nature of our experiences and character. Sometimes even the simplest of observations can spark insightful meditations like this that challenge us to re-examine our presuppositions and usual modes of thinking—like the reminder that in one sense unsupervised experiences are an illusion, since, as we have seen, there has never been a moment when we have not been under the careful superintending watch and concern of the One who put us here in the first place, who holds our very breath and heartbeat in His hands. And if this doesn't bring a helpful dose of sobriety to our overall outlook, informing how we engage with this world and one another, I'm not sure what will.

Another important reminder that this thought experiment yields is that, when it comes to a subject like this, we are neither adequately equipped, nor required, to understand how the whole program works on the deepest levels, including the need to account for all the reasons why negative, destructive, painful experiences have for so long been allowed to come to pass. Even if we were allowed to know more fully why certain things, or even all of them, have been permitted, maybe we would be worse off for knowing this. Maybe the less we know, the better. In fact, doesn't it make more sense to think that the ways, motives, and capabilities of such a Being must necessarily be far beyond those of His creatures, as Scripture plainly and repeatedly indicates?

For my thoughts are not your thoughts,

> neither are your ways my ways, declares the LORD.
> For as the heavens are higher than the earth,
>> so are my ways higher than your ways
>> and my thoughts than your thoughts.[16]

Pondering the ontological possibilities along these lines, old Anselm was onto something with his simple but profound "that than which nothing greater can be thought." Standing on the same distant shore as he, we can only trace the horizon so far, glimpsing things "in a mirror dimly."[17] We can only do so much to piece together the outer border of the puzzle, which holds everything else together. But rather than feeling frustrated and beaten down by the persistent reign of evil and chaos in the world, no matter how close to home it hits, we can rest assured that this is only temporary and is being allowed for very particular reasons, the motives for which will ultimately be vindicated as just. More than that, before we know it the Great Day will come when the King of kings and Lord of lords will make all things right and put them in their proper place, when the full panorama of the mysterious masterpiece will be unveiled and magnified in all its intricate splendor, when faith once and for all gives way to sight.

---

[1] Matt. 13:24-30

[2] While this subpoint deviates slightly from the initial question regarding things we *once* did of which we now disapprove, to the effects that *all* of our good and bad unsupervised experiences have had on us regardless of whether or not we now approve, this should not be construed as the same thing as the initial question, though it is related.

[3] C. S. Lewis, *Mere Christianity* (HarperCollins, New York, 2001), 9.

[4] Ibid, 25.

[5] Ibid, 9.

[6] Gen. 37, 39-50

[7] Gen. 37:2; 41:46; 45:6

[8] Gen. 50:20

[9] Gen. 45:4-8

[10] Acts 2:22-23

[11] Thomas Aquinas, *Summa Contra Gentiles*, trans. Vernon J. Bourke (University of Notre Dame Press, Notre Dame), 3a 72.2.

[12] Rom. 11:33, 36

[13] Luke 7:36-50

[14] Acts 9:1-2; 22:4-5, 19-20; 26:9-11; Gal. 1:13

[15] 1 Cor. 15:9; Gal. 1:13; Eph. 3:8; 1 Tim. 1:15

[16] Isa. 55:8-9

[17] 1 Cor. 13:12

Available from Amazon.com, Kindle, and other retail outlets

THIS WAS
JUST THE WAY

A Memoir

TED STAMP

Made in United States
Troutdale, OR
08/11/2023